Bill,

   We hope when you browse through this book it will always remind you of your good friends in Texas.

   May our companies continue the successful partnerships we've had for many years to come.

Paul Finley

Richard Hart

Ken Dickey

Jim H Thompson

Don Ashley

Ashley Clark

The Big Thicket: Many years ago longleaf
yellow pine was the dominant timber in the Big
Thicket; this was eradicated by lumbering. The
trees that remain are mostly hardwoods.
These, and brush, create a series of small
thickets, which, however, give the impression
of being one immense jungle.

Texas

A salute from above

Text by T. R. Fehrenbach

Photography by

Bill Ellzey   George Hall   Charles O'Rear   Tony Weissgarber

PORTLAND HOUSE
New York

Text by T. R. Fehrenbach
Photography by Bill Ellzey, George Hall,
Charles O'Rear and Tony Weissgarber

Publishers: Kevin Weldon, John Owen
Managing Editor: Mary-Dawn Earley
Project Coordinator: Christine Joy Smith
John Owen
Research: Gus Clemens
Design: Adrian Young
Production: Cecille Weldon

Weldon Owen Inc.,
3rd Floor, 90 Gold Street,
San Francisco CA 94133, USA
Tel (415) 291 0100 Fax (415) 291 8841

This 1988 edition (reprinted 1990)
published by Portland House,
distributed by Outlet Book Company Inc.,
A Random House Company,
225 Park Avenue South,
New York, New York 10003

Printed by Griffin Press, Netley,
South Australia, 5037, Australia.

Library of Congress Catalog Card
Number 84-52739

ISBN 0-517-66469-0

9 8 7 6 5 4 3 2

Endpapers
Field near Haskell, West Texas.

Pages 2-3
Rio Grande

Pages 4-5
Small lake, Henderson County near Athens,
North Texas

This page
Texas soil near Shamrock, on the eastern edge of
the Panhandle: The earth itself is still the most
significant feature of Texas, dominating even man. It
is still the source of most of the state's riches.

*With special thanks to
Continental Airlines.*

ACKNOWLEDGEMENTS
The photographers would like to thank the
following people who gave them great
assistance and support in this project;
Ricky Anderson, Matt Baker, Joe Bowman,
Augusta Clark, Elden Criswell, Jens
Dissing, Glen and Mary Jane Eller, Jerry
Fletcher, Bill Harris, Rosanne Henna,
Harrison Knapp, Dan Landis, Carl
Lange, Harper Leiper, Jerry
Livanec, Clarence Lott, Mike
Marvins, Greg Pitts, Sandra
Provenzano, Gary Pry, True
and Lady Margaret Redd,
Doug Soltau and Bob Trick.

Printed in Australia

Contents

Foreword

Look with new eyes upon Texas.
Its sweeping diversity is seen from
another perspective — the view from
above.
From the canyons of the Big Bend to the dense forest
of East Texas, from the endless wheatfields of the
Panhandle to the bright beaches of the Gulf Coast —
Texas is here.
Our state's towns and cities are here, too, from
Terlingua to Houston and Amarillo to Brownsville.
All of it is captured in magnificent color by America's
leading aerial photographers.
Ted Fehrenbach, a San Antonian who knows and loves
Texas, recreates the state's history with a keen eye for
detail and an understanding of the saga of its growth.
Texas — A Salute From Above is a fresh and unusual
concept which erases the cliches and allows the reader
to see the real Texas.

Mark White
Governor of Texas
1983 – 1987

A Methodist Church in Wichita Falls.

The Guadalupe Mountains: A remnant of primordial Texas, the Guadalupes are the highest mountains in the state. Guadalupe Peak (8,749 feet) is the highest peak east of the Rockies. Because of the perspective from the plain it is overshadowed by El Capitan (8,085 feet), which dominates the countryside for 40 miles. This was a major landmark for nineteenth-century travelers west, and a spectacle for passengers on the Butterfield Stage.

New houses on Abilene's west side: This new construction in Abilene, a booming West Texas oil centre, symbolizes the impact of present population growth and development across the state.

Introduction

Some time ago I wrote of Texas: *In the beginning, before any people, was the land: an immense region 265,000 square miles in area rising out of the warm muck of the green Gulf of Mexico, running for countless leagues of rich coastal prairies, forests, and savannahs; reaching out hugely 770 miles from boundary to boundary south to north and east to west, to enclose a series of magnificent, rising limestone plateaus, ending in the thin, hot air of blue-shadowed mountains.*

That, of course, is a word picture. Now, the art of the photographer has captured what I tried to do with language, in the timeless quality of Texas' shores, vast prairies, and mountains. But it has done more than that; it has also captured the vibrant, colorful, ever-changing civilization men have impressed upon the land, from sprawling cities to lonely tractors carving furrows across the western plain. The photographs reveal Texas in a way it has never been revealed before.

No matter how familiar the viewer may be with the state of Texas, how much of it he may have visited, ridden or walked over, or even flown over, in this book are scenes he will never have seen. This is an eagle's eye view of Texas, and it shows the state as no other method or literature can, visually and viscerally.

The concept and practice of above-ground photography is not new, but no one has applied it to the whole state of Texas before this book. The reason is simple enough: Texas is a huge place, and no one was willing to send helicopters or balloons to all corners of the state, taking 10,000 photographs from which to select a few hundred to be printed. It was an enormous and chancy undertaking, full of potential foul-ups and frustrations. The result is a stunning product, Texas — A Salute from Above, that gives both Texans and non-Texans a new and entirely wonderful perspective of this state.

The perspective is not of Texas as it was but Texas as it is today.

Texas is no longer the mere prospect of an empire but an empire indeed, a land and people having more than local importance. However, most books about Texas are backward-looking, exploring or locked into the past. Most Texas literature, even most Texas photography, tries to refurbish, embellish, or preserve the Texas past. But while the Texas past is a vital history that gives Texans their sense of identity and their deep feeling for time and place, the thrust of a rapidly changing Texas is toward the future.

Texas is a place with ancient glories, a magnificent, turbulent present, and an incredible future.

These pictures catch all these realities. They show the timeless nature of the land, the ceaseless, restless action of the people, burgeoning, building, destroying and restoring.

The photographs express the sheer immensity of this state. The land dominates in many places in an almost Russian sense. Texas is vast: as large as New York, Pennsylvania, Ohio, and Illinois with all New England thrown in besides; larger than North and South Carolina, Georgia, Florida, and Alabama combined. Its territory exceeds that of many nations; South Texas alone is bigger than England and Wales.

The early settlers, like the English who first saw Australia, found little beauty in the Texas landscape. It took succeeding generations in both places to understand both the eternal beauty and fragility of such soil. These pictures show us both the wildness of Texas nature, and also a country where the artifacts of man still appear as specks on the desolate horizon.

We tend to think of Texas and the Southwest as an old land, where eons ago Permian forests decayed into gigantic pools of oil, where Indians roamed for thousands of years, and invading Spaniards explored and made lonely outposts. This view is true, but in terms of today's reality, it is increasingly meaningless. Texas' civilization is very new. The true frontier is not that of vanished cowboys and Indians, but the technological culture pushing into the next century.

Open range outside Alpine: For many people around the world, great open spaces — where prairie and mountains meet the sky — symbolize Texas, where the West began.

The state of Texas is one of the fastest growing and changing areas of the world. Great, sparkling cities have sprung up almost overnight from forlorn frontier stations and trading posts. These cities are shining beads strung across the dark thread of the land. Many are old in the dates of their founding. San Antonio and El Paso rightly take pride in an antiquity that is quite respectable on the North American continent. The truth, however, is that all Texas cities must be seen as very new, twentieth-century creations of the automobile and air age, ultra-modern in technique, and just now moving into world rank and importance.

Texas is still advancing across its prairies, still spreading out hugely, still a-making, still forcing civilization upon a stubborn soil. For better or for worse, Texans are still engaged in battle on and with this, their chosen land, forging a state that now impacts strongly on the greater nation and even the world. Texas once might have been considered quaint or eccentric, a relic of the old frontier. Today, its factories, farms, and universities are blazing new trails into the future.

Texas, of course, is more than just another administrative unit of the American Union. It is more than merely the largest of the contiguous continental forty-eight states. In a way no other American state quite matches, Texas is also a state of heart and mind.

Like France and Israel, Texas has both a history and mystique.

Alone among the American states it was once its own nation, born like most historic nations in blood and iron. Texas had the bloodiest and longest running frontiers in American history, something others forget. Out of the crucible of this nineteenth-century experience, out of a chemistry of culture and struggle, Texans emerged very much a people, American to the core but still at the very least a conscious subculture within the United States.

Texas had to battle Mexico for freedom, making its own hallowed ground. Texans fought Indians for the land, and then the land itself for survival. They made war against the greater nation itself in the name of independence. And for generations, Texans were at the sharp end of the advance of civilization across the continent. Texas was the key to the conquest of that continent; without Texas the history of the United States itself is unthinkable. And long after all the wars were ended, the old frontier and frontier conditions lingered longer in Texas than almost anywhere else.

From this came the Texan mystique — proud, part myth, part truth about the land and people. It is a mystique that holds a huge, complex, and varied region together. The Texas mystique makes Texas more than just an area drawn upon the map. Take those arbitrary boundaries away, and Texas would remain Texas in the minds of all its citizens.

Under the terms of the treaty of annexation by the United States, Texas reserves the right to divide into five separate states. This notion is occasionally broached — the idea of having ten Texas senators in Washington confronting the Yankees has its attractions — but this has never happened and never will. The notion of Texas overpowers all other notions. Even the most Southwestern-oriented El Pasoan doing business only in New Mexico, the most alienated border dweller, and the most Deep-South denizen of the Piney Woods hesitates to make such a psychological secession.

Texans do not call themselves East Texans, South Texans, or West Texans to outlanders, no more than they think of themselves as Houstonians or Dallasites. They are first and last Texans, who may come from some remote part or happen to live in another. They are Americans who are Texans in the same way some Britons are Scots and some Germans are Bavarians — and proud of it.

Non-Texans should not make too much of the regional and cosmetic differences between the widely separated parts of Texas, nor of those between city and countryside. The great Texas cities, true metropolises, are yet far too new to have created a true, parochial, urban culture such as the older cities of Europe and America. Nor are they yet urbane. They rise up from and sprawl across the plains and then merge back into them. In some similar fashion, their inhabitants live in a sort of two-way osmosis between country and town. The country is never quite removed from the urban Texan, and he remains close to it for renewal.

In this way, the new Texas and Southwestern city has not repeated many of the cultural and social patterns of older cities elsewhere. It blends town and country. It creates mindsets, or perhaps, fails to change mindsets, that are closer to rural America than those of Eastern or Northern city-dwellers.

This has made a Texas citizenry, 80 percent of whom live in urban or metropolitan areas, that seem uniquely comfortable and at home both in the city and on the land, in glass towers or in the saddle, or even on man's ultimate frontier, space.

There are many books on Texas, and there will be many more. But this book, I think, will be forever valuable for it has caught Texas at a vital point in time, the day of its true emergence from hardship and heartbreak into an American empire. This book, these pictures, these words, are about what Texas *is*.

It is the present that will be our past tomorrow — a thing even historians at times forget.

In this book I have divided Texas into a number of arbitrary geographic divisions for convenience. There are many different ways of dividing Texas into parts: the purely geographic, based on climate, soils, and topography; the historic; and the emotional and sentimental. But since the great geographic regions merge almost imperceptibly into each other — most Texans cannot tell you where the South Plains or Western Plains begin or end — and residents of some Texas towns argue whether or not they live in "West Texas," I have used my own combination of all methods. There is, actually, no standard cartographic system that separates Texas neatly by area or region.

Further, I have not tried to break the state down into every possible region and subregion, such as "Brush

Country," "Hill Country," or "Post-oak Belt." These places all fall within larger geographic areas and such delineations would become tedious and confusing.

The headings used, such as the division of the immense West Texas area, 40 per cent of the state, into three broad regions, separating the Trans-Pecos region and the Panhandle, calling the remainder "West Texas" may offend some purists and some local sensibilities. But this is easily understood by Texans and non-Texans alike and makes as much sense as any other system.

This, then, is Texas: Texas as it was and as it is, with some hints as to what it will be.

It's a magnificent view of a magnificent country, and I hope it will help the viewer to a greater understanding of why we Texans love it.

T.R.F.

Texas-sized swimming pool, Williams Ranch, Alpine.

The Trans-Pecos Region

The Trans-Pecos Region, which geographers call the "Western Mountains and Basins Region" is just that: the land west of the Pecos River, a huge region larger than many nations, bounded on the north by New Mexico and on the south by the Rio Grande and Mexico. The eastern portion is the rolling plain and rough country of the Pecos Valley and the Stockton Plateau. The rest is crossed by two mountain ranges (the only true mountains in Texas) and basins, each of which has its own name. The mountains are really outcroppings of the Rockies.

To the east lie the Guadalupe, Davis, Ord, Santiago, Corazones, Rosillos, and Chisos Mountains. The western line of mountains includes the Heucos, Finlays, Quitmans, Eagles, Viejos, and Chinatis. In between, not quite connected to either, lies the Sierra Diablo. The individual names given these ranges and sierras are confusing; non-natives are rarely certain which mountains they are traversing. No matter. Each range, each peak, is steeped in song and story, and avid readers of Western novels over the years will recognize most of the names. Many tales of the wild West and many a John Wayne movie have been set in these mountains.

West of the Guadalupes lies Diablo (Devil) Basin, a vast plateau with no drainage, covered with ephemeral salt lakes. When these burn off in dry spells, their bottoms become solid salt — salt that was once mined and over which men killed in the 1870s.

This is a country of vast spaces, incredible harshness and loneliness, and monumental spectacle. It is arid; rainfall averages only 10–12 inches annually. It is a land of stark contrasts: salt basins and semi-deserts, high flat-topped mesas capped with volcanic rock, great buttes of igneous stone, soaring mountains covered with great trees. Some of the mountains are reefs of ancient seas; others were made by volcanic action. All of them seem to leap suddenly from the sandy plain, sometimes singly, usually an entire sierra or saw-toothed range. The summits are sharp, outlined against a burning sky, interspersed with rounded domes and deeply etched ravines.

The country is given to extremes — blazing heat in summer, icy winds in winter.

This has always been a kingdom remote from most of Texas. The Republic of Texas (1836–46) claimed the Rio Grande as its boundary although American settlement had nowhere approached that river at the time. The boundary was confirmed by the Treaty of Guadalupe Hidalgo that ended the Mexican War (1848), although the United States refused to accede Texas those lands east of the river that are now New Mexico. The Trans-Pecos, in fact, like all West Texas, was still Indian country.

The first stage line, en route to California, and the first white settlement pushed across the Pecos in the 1850s. The nature of settlement, based on the nature of the land, was the formation of vast, remote cattle ranches, isolated baronies whose headquarters stood like feudal castles, armed against marauding Apaches and no less dangerous raiders from south of the Rio Grande. In the 1880s the railroads connected the Pecos country with the state and nation and made a few towns. But for 50 years there was not much change.

This has come mainly in the last generation, with new highways and airports, parks and visitors, colleges and satellite-broadcast TV. There is law west of the Pecos now; Judge Roy Bean no longer holds court with rope and six-gun. Isolated ranches are no longer fortresses, and cowhands, at least since 1940, no longer ride pistol-heavy into town.

But much of the past remains. The towns across this vast expanse of earth and sky are still mostly small frontier outposts staked out bravely against the deepening West. The great ranches still have the aura of independent principalities, which the owners sometimes refer to as their "countries." The land itself, away from those portions near the Pecos River and on the Stockton Plateau where the discovery of deep underground water some years back led to the farming of grain and alfalfa, has hardly been scratched by the hand of man.

This is still a land of remote ranches and mines, a land of haunting harshness and haunting beauty, a land of legend.

Its history still lies all about in the ruins of other years. Its future, however, has hardly begun.

Below and overleaf The Davis Mountains: Long the haunt of Apaches, these mountains — like most things in Jeff Davis County — were named for the Mississippian secretary of war in the 1850s. Davis, who had studied the experience of the French Foreign Legion in the Sahara Desert, had a vast interest in the "Great American Desert," as the West was then called. He organized the first U.S. cavalry regiment and imported camels for service in Texas as well as establishing frontier outposts.

Antonio de Bermejo and party passed this way in 1583, but the Spanish never colonized the area.

The mountains run some 50 miles north-northwest from Fort Davis and are about 40 miles wide. They are formed mainly of red rock thrust upward by volcanic action, with much twisting and turning. The principal peaks include Mounts Livermore (8,382 feet), Sawtooth (7,748), and Blue (7,330). Mount Locke (6,791) holds the famous McDonald Observatory.

GEORGE HALL

Downtown Marfa: Marfa, seat of Presidio County in the Big Bend, has two claims to fame: the movie "Giant" was filmed near here, and it may be the only town in America named for a character in a Russian novel. The wife of the chief engineer of the Texas and New Orleans Railroad was reading Dostoevski's *The Brothers Karamazov* when the rails reached here in 1881. When a water stop was placed on the spot, the site was named at her whim — Marfa, of course, being a servant in the Karamazov household. Marfa became the seat of the new county in 1885, and the three-storeyed courthouse built in 1886 is still in use, along with the restored old Paisano Hotel.

Although the town has declined from a population of about 4,000 in 1930 to the present 2,466 (1980), it is still an important crossroads at the juncture of Highways 90 and 67. Highway 67 leads to the Big Bend National Park and the border village of Presidio, making Marfa a jumping off place for Mexico. Mysterious lights seen in the mountains around Marfa have been ascribed to UFOs and extra-terrestrial visitors; more likely they are the results of plasma creation in an area of ongoing geologic activity.

Right

The town of Fort Davis, adjacent to the preserved fort, grew up alongside it. It became the seat of Jeff Davis County. However, the town remained small; some 900 people reside there today. Fort Davis has an abundance of fine old houses and buildings, including the once-famed Limpia Hotel, the 1910 courthouse, and an old drugstore that still serves fountain Coca Cola made from syrup. A resort, and a magnet for tourists on the road, the town comes alive in summer and during various holidays.

Overleaf

Fort Davis: In the 1850s this spot on Limpia (Clean) Creek was selected for a stage stop on the California run. In 1854 Secretary of War Jefferson Davis, who was extremely interested in the West, established an Army post to offer protection to the travelers. The fort was built on land leased from John James of San Antonio, whose family retained ownership until the site was purchased in 1961 by the National Parks Service.

The first Fort Davis was constructed from timber cut in the surrounding Davis Mountains, where there is plenty of yellow and limber pine. When the fort was abandoned by the Army during the Civil War, the Apaches immediately burned it to the ground. However, when the soldiers returned in 1867, they built a new fort farther down the canyon, this time of stone and adobe. From 1881 to 1891, when it was finally closed, Fort Davis was headquarters for the Department of the Pecos. Colonel Benjamin H. Grierson, noted for "Grierson's Raid" during the Civil War and as commander for the all-black Tenth Cavalry Regiment in the Comanche campaigns, commanded here until his retirement in 1890. After the post was abandoned, squatters moved in and the facilities gradually fell into disrepair. During the 1930s local residents made some efforts toward preservation, and in 1961 the federal government declared Fort Davis a National Historic Site. By the late 1960s, it had been restored to its exact 1880 state and appearance. As a splendid example of a frontier Western cavalry post, it receives hundreds of thousands of visitors each year.

GEORGE HALL

The McDonald Observatory, Mount Locke, Davis Mountains: In 1926 William Johnson McDonald bequeathed to the University of Texas money to create an observatory. The site chosen was a 6,791-foot peak northwest of Fort Davis, where atmospheric conditions and remoteness are ideal. The ground on Mount Locke was donated by Violet Locke McIvor of New Hampshire, daughter of the Texas pioneer for whom it was named. The facility was not completed and dedicated, however, until May 5, 1939.

Until 1963 the McDonald Observatory was operated under a special agreement by the University of Chicago; since then the University of Texas has assumed full control. The McDonald has some of the most advanced and sophisticated astronomical equipment in the world, including 82-inch and 107-inch reflector telescopes and various radio telescopes. It is able to bounce a laser beam with the power of a billion photons from the moon, measuring the exact distance from earth to moon and establishing the extent of continental drift here on earth.

In the planning stage is a 300-inch reflector telescope, which would be the largest anywhere. The Soviets have one that size, but reportedly it does not work because of design failures.

Overleaf

Terlingua, ghost town: There is general agreement that the name Terlingua stands for "three tongues" or "three languages." But no one knows just which three: Spanish, Comanche, Apache, or Spanish, English, Seminole — or some combination with sign language. It probably no longer matters: Terlingua is what is known in the West as a ghost town. Everybody left long ago when the mines shut down.

Great deposits of cinnabar were found here in the 1890s, making Texas a prime producer of quicksilver, or mercury, for 40 years. However, both the deposits and the market for mercury gradually failed, and the town barely held on through World War II. Finally, both were abandoned in the 1940s.

Such histories are common in the mountains of the American West; ores and markets play out over the years; buildings survive in the desiccated climate. Terlingua, however, because of its proximity to Big Bend National Park has seen a number of real estate and other promotions. The World Championship Chili Cook-off brings 5,000 visitors each fall, keeping Terlingua on the map.

However, the normal population, including sales agents, is 25; the real metropolis of the area is Study Butte (population 120). Visitors should inquire first before going there.

Geologically speaking, the Big Bend (so named from the great loop the border river makes down into Mexico) is a crossroads, where the Rocky Mountain and Appalachia Uplifts converge. This has created some of the most spectacular scenery anywhere and an ecology that is unique on the North American continent. The Big Bend, like the Trans-Pecos Region generally, combines an unusual geology, fauna, and flora not found anywhere else. The high mountains grow both Rocky Mountain cedars and large Texas oaks, cottonwoods and black cherrywoods and pines. The smaller shrubbery shows the same blend. The wildlife includes antelope, black bear, mule deer (and in the higher Chisos the rare Del Carmen white-tails), bobcat, cougar and bighorn sheep, along with all the chipmunks, rabbits, skunks, rats, gophers, squirrels, opossums, porcupines, and other varmints good and bad that inhabit less exotic climes.

The Big Bend was almost a foreign kingdom not long ago. Few roads entered it; habitations were few and far between. The land was taken up in huge private holdings whose owners or managers, true to the Texan ethos, were as apt to reach for a Winchester as to hail a stranger traversing their range.

Texas, unlike other Western states, has never contained any federal or public lands. The 1845 treaty of annexation reserved all public lands to the state, and the state quickly sold them off — often while these were still the hunting grounds of Indians. Ever since, whenever either the United States government or the State of Texas acquires land in Texas, it must be purchased or received as a gift.

Until 1943 there had never been a federal park or parkland in the state.

GEORGE HALL

When World War II opened up the Trans-Pecos with new roads and visitors, new attention was focused on the priceless wilderness heritage of the whole area and especially the Big Bend country. In 1943 Big Bend National Park was created through an immense donation of land, 788,682 acres in the wildest section of the Chisos Mountains beside the border. This park is still remote, but it draws thousands of visitors to its remarkable topography and ecology.

The favorite area of the park for tourists — who may ride or hike over a wilderness unchanged in 1,000 years — are the canyons and gorges cut through the native rock by the Rio Grande. In the back country the greenhorn may always encounter a rattlesnake, but the canyons offer fast water and remarkable scenery.

These are the Grand Canyons of Santa Elena, Mariscal, and Boquillas. In recent geological time, 50,000 to 100,000 years ago, the river created a vast lake and tropical swamp region here. Finally the waters broke through the Chisos barrier at Boquillas Canyon, draining the basins, while the Rio Grande cut a deep path through the rock from basin to basin. In historic times Santa Elena Canyon played a grimmer historic role. This was one of the two major passageways for the Comanche Indians into Mexico. The Trans-Pecos was not Comanche range; they lived on the high bison plains of West Texas, driving the Apaches into these mountains. But they rode through regularly on raiding parties into northern Mexico where in the nineteenth century they caused widespread devastation. The United States pledged to try to halt this in the Treaty

of Guadalupe Hidalgo. This was a principal reason, along with the protection of stage travelers, for stationing soldiers in the region. In the days when the stretches of the upper Rio Grande were a lush tropical paradise, various Indian peoples — now unknown except from their artifacts — lived in caves beside the river. They created artwork on the walls similar to that made by Cro-Magnon dwellers in the Pyrenees.

Unless and until the ecology of the region changes again, only a few people will ever live in the Big Bend country beside the Rio Grande — or anywhere else in these plains and mountains. Their stark beauty, however, has been preserved while they have been made accessible to man — no small triumph for the state and nation.

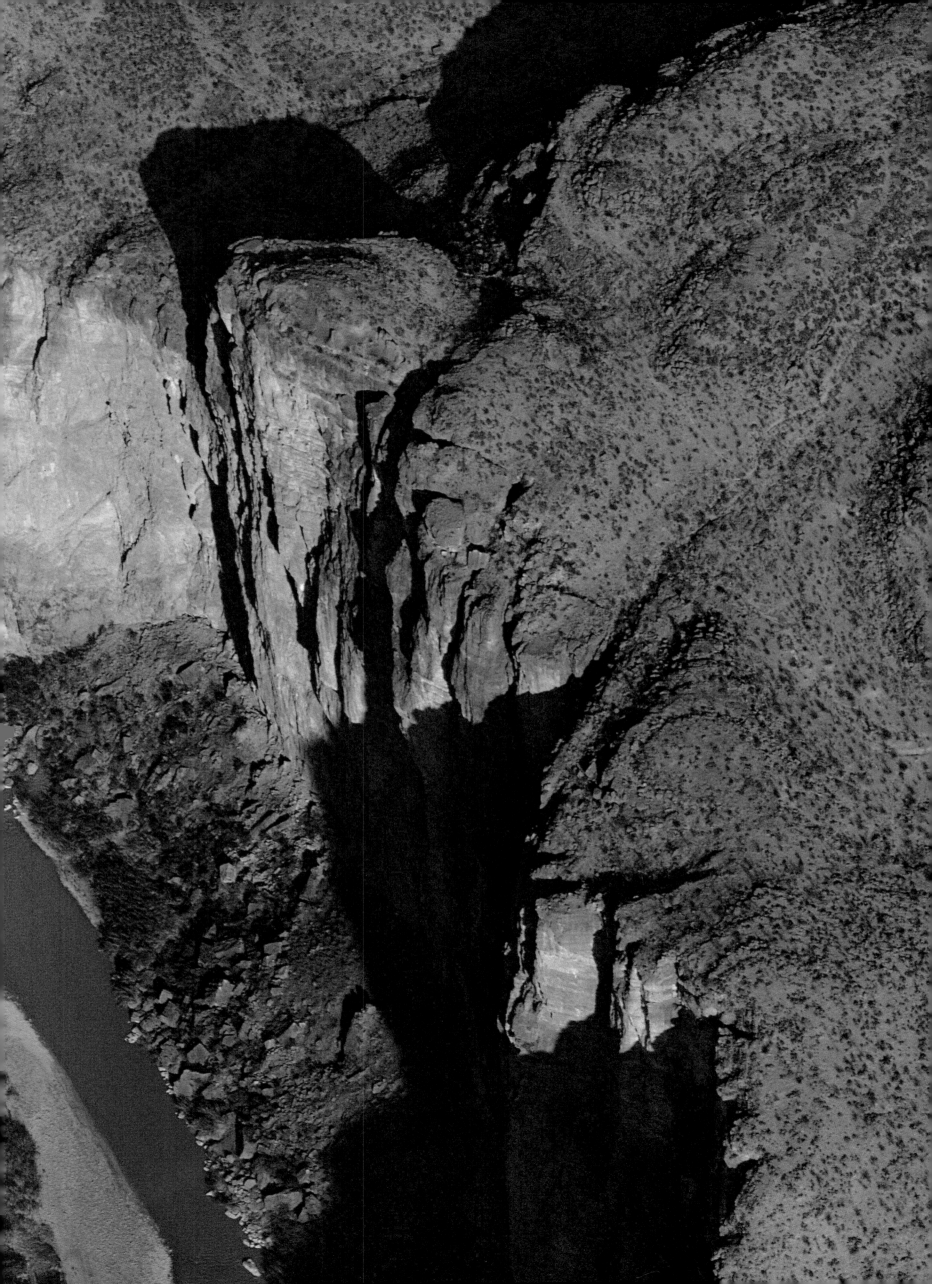

GEORGE HALL

GEORGE HALL

Left

The Van Horn Mountains: The mountains rise in the southwestern corner of Culberson County south of the town of Van Horn (visible from Interstate 10), west of Lobo and Wild Horse Creek. They run for about 20 miles, the highest peaks reaching just over 5,000 feet. They are named for James Judson Van Horn, a young West Point graduate who commanded an Army post near Lobo in 1859. Van Horn later served at Fort Davis 1859–1861; he was held a prisoner of war by the Confederates until 1862. Despite his adventures in war and Indian country, Van Horn died peacefully in 1898. The Van Horns are not, as many Texans believe, named for Jefferson Van Horne, the Mexican War hero who blazed the first trail — the Military or Lower Road — from San Antonio to El Paso in 1849, although the town of Van Horn lies on it.

In all respects, the Van Horns are typical of the more rugged sierras of the Trans-Pecos, with great rock faces and deeply cut ravines.

GEORGE HALL

Above

Indian Hot Springs: Indian Hot Springs is a resort on Quitman Arroyo of the Rio Grande, downstream from Fort Quitman in the southernmost foothills of the mountains. Facilities are sparse: There is a hotel and dining room and not much else, but people come here to see the country and for the hot baths. Like most places in the Big Bend, the resort has a patina of age and history. Hundreds of hot springs flow from this area into the Rio Grande. After the Texas Pacific and Southern Pacific Railroads met at Sierra Blanca in 1881, the baths were opened to the hot and dusty traveling public.

The "hot springs" all along the river are mostly seeps, trickles of water that accumulate in rock pools. The water is pure, coming from aquifers in the rocks, and it is heated principally by the normal radioactivity of the earth.

Left

The Quitman Mountains: The Quitmans are a dry, rugged sierra that hugs the Mexican border in southern Hudspeth County. They reach a height of 6,500 feet. These mountains are pocked with mines old and new; if the silver and mercury are now played out, zinc is still found in large quantities. Much of the zinc produced in Texas comes from the Quitmans. The only town nearby, Sierra Blanca, is north of the range. Sierra Blanca draws its name from a large, gypsum-colored mountain nearby. Old Fort Quitman on the Rio Grande lies on what is now designated as Farm Road 192. There is a passage through the mountains that leads down to the river; this is known as Quitman Pass.

Right and below right

The Guadalupe Mountains: Unlike many of the ranges in the Trans-Pecos, the Guadalupes are not the result of vulcanism; they are the remains of great reefs of the Permian seas more than 200 million years ago, now turned into solid limestone. They guard the vast Permian basin extending east to south, an ancient sea bed that now produces more than 20 percent of U.S. natural gas and petroleum. The mountains present an extremely dramatic appearance, especially when approached from the south. They are very rugged, also; they were one of the last refuges of the Apache Indians in the 1880s. They extend north across the New Mexico border; the famous Carlsbad Caverns are Permian reefs carved by water action into the largest limestone caves in the world.

The Guadalupes are accessible at the Guadalupe Mountains National Park. This was established in 1963, the first national park obtained principally through purchase (by Wallace Pratt, a geologist who willed the government his holdings in McKittrick Canyon).

McKittrick Canyon contains an extraordinary range of geologic features, fauna, climate, and vegetation. Desert, forest, and mountain environments can be experienced in a single hike. The interior portion of the park is considered one of the best-preserved wilderness areas in the United States. However, it is reached only by hard climbing. Access is restricted to experienced backpackers. No fires are allowed; there are no food, water, or rescue services, and whatever a camper carries in he must prove he carried out.

GEORGE HALL

Above

El Paso: El Paso is where both the Trans-Pecos and Texas end. Nestled between the Rockies on the west and the Organ Mountains north and east, the city is closer to Los Angeles than to Texarkana — which in turn is closer to Chicago than to El Paso.

Many El Pasoans think of themselves as more "Southwestern" than Texan. Geographically, economically, historically, and culturally, the city has more in common with New Mexico than Texas.

El Paso has a long, varied, and sometimes violent, past. It began as *El Paso del Norte,* the lowest-elevation all-weather passageway through the Continental Divide, which the Spanish discovered on their way to New Mexico in 1598. Missions, trading posts, and forts followed; today El Paso is a city of nearly half a million people, fourth-largest in Texas, with a metropolitan area including more than a million people if the Mexican sister city of Juarez is included. Nearby Fort Bliss, which has switched from cavalry mounts to anti-aircraft missiles, contains more territory than Rhode Island.

El Paso considers itself the city of five "Cs": cattle, copper, cotton, clothing and climate. All are important to its vibrant Sunbelt economy, but climate may be its proudest boast. Reputedly the sun has only failed to shine here 23 days in the last fourteen years.

GEORGE HALL

GEORGE HALL

The Panhandle

The Panhandle gets its name from the handle-like appearance of Texas' far-northwestern boundaries on the map. Topographically, the western and major portion of the Panhandle is part of the Great High Plains running along the eastern base of the Rockies, the largest level land area of its kind in the United States. The eastern edge of the Panhandle falls within the Rolling Plains, part of the North Central Plains of Texas. The land above and west of the Cap Rock Escarpment, which divides the High and Rolling Plains, is called the Llano Estacado. This is a high, dry, treeless plain, some of the flattest land on Earth. It rises from about 2,700 feet in the east to about 4,000 feet along the New Mexico border.

The Great High Plains of Texas is divided into two subsections running north to south, the North and South Plains. These merge into each other imperceptibly around Plainview in Hale County; the main reason for a demarcation is that there are subtle climatic differences that make the South Plains the center of Texas cotton farming. The true Panhandle region, lying to the north, though it grows much cotton is primarily devoted to wheat and sorghum production, along with significant ranching and petroleum.

One can easily argue about where the Panhandle ends and the South Plains begins. However, this expanse was once part of that "sea of grass" that overwhelmed the first Europeans — vast savannahs of tall, rustling grasses that rolled ocean-like from the Cross Timbers west of Fort Worth to the high plateaus.

The Panhandle, especially the Llano Estacado, held the highest concentration of American bison or buffalo in North America. These hunting grounds were held and defended against other Indians and white men by the fiercest of the Plains tribes, the Kwahadi Comanches. They were virtually unknown to Americans before the last quarter of the nineteenth century. As late as 1876 there was no permanent Texas settlement north of Big Spring, where the Cap Rock Escarpment begins; the Great High Plains was an unmapped wilderness crossed only by buffalo hunters and the cavalry, both at their peril.

When the Comanches were defeated and removed to the Indian Territory in 1874–5, however, white appropriation of the country took place explosively. The last of the southern buffalo herds were soon slaughtered for their hides; cattlemen cut up the country into vast pastures.

Two inventions, windmills and barbed wire, permitted the plains to be seized by stockmen. The first were necessary to draw up good ground water for man and beast. Surface water in the Panhandle is seasonal and ephemeral, the shallow lakes drying up in the blast of summer; most of the small rivers and streams are so choked by gypsum or so alkaline as to be undrinkable. The second, while it doomed the open range over the often violent and bloody protests of some pioneers, made possible a true cattle industry based on improved breeds. Because of British interest and investment in far-west Texas, Herefords and other heavy breeds were soon introduced from the British Isles, replacing the longhorns, a Mexican-derived half-wild range stock.

While the country was quickly carved into great ranches and railroads began to push through — during the last quarter of the century there were many small railroad companies, each building its own lines — and settlements sprouted alongside the tracks, full development proceeded slowly. For many years the Panhandle remained a land of vast cattle ranches, while the proximity of the New Mexico and Indian Territory (Oklahoma) and Colorado lines encouraged widespread cattle rustling. During the first decade of the twentieth century, the battles between cattle thieves and range detectives resembled a war.

Stratford at sunset: Stratford, a town of about 2,000, lies high on the wheat lands along the Oklahoma line. The seat of Sherman County — which has only some 3,000 inhabitants — is characteristic of the Panhandle, a land of vast horizons, few people, and immense farms. Stratford (on Coldwater Creek) was named by Walter Colton, an Englishman, for Stratford-on-Avon. The resemblance ends with the name. Founded in 1885, Stratford-on-Coldwater did not become the county seat until the railroad arrived in 1900. Even then the competition was so fierce that county records had to be protected by armed guards.

Old headquarters of the XIT Ranch at Buffalo Springs: The XIT is probably the most famous cattle brand in Texas and the West. It has a colorful, complex history. A Chicago firm, Taylor, Babcock & Co., accepted 3.5 million acres in the Panhandle from the Texas Legislature in payment for construction of the Texas Capitol in the 1880s. The Chicagoans never intended to go into the ranching business, but they had to develop the land in order to sell it profitably. To raise capital for ranching operations, bonds were sold in London, where American ranching investments were very fashionable.

The XIT holdings covered ten Panhandle counties. Between 1885–1900, 1,500 miles of wire was strung, the ranch divided into 94

42 ☆ TEXAS – A SALUTE FROM ABOVE

great divisions or pastures. The ranch began to be sold off in 1901, George W. Littlefield buying 225,858 acres in one parcel. Much of the land, however, went to farmers. The last of the XIT cattle were sold in 1912, and the last ranch lands in 1950.

The XIT brand, sometimes fabled as "Ten in Texas," had no real symbolism; it was chosen by Ab Blocker, the manager, because it was simple and relatively difficult for rustlers to blot or burn out. But the brand impressed itself permanently on the territory. The city of Dalhart is still "XIT country"; Hartley and Dallam counties maintain an XIT Museum; and the symbol is still seen everywhere.

The XIT was the greatest of its kind, and its mark still lives.

Below

Perryton: Eight miles south of the Oklahoma border, Perryton is the seat of Ochiltree County in the heart of the high wheat belt. From the air, like most High Plains settlements, it appears a crossroads planted in the endless land. It was named for George M. Perry, early settler and county judge.

Right Highway 54: U.S. Highway 54 runs between Dalhart and Stratford, crossing the northwest corner of the Panhandle — and a lot of nowhere. Travelers in Texas are often startled by the quality of the highways: there are good paved roads in every corner of the state — and what other states might call prime highways sometimes lead only to isolated farms or ranches. With 250,000 miles of municipal and rural highways, Texas leads all other states. In fact, it has more paved road than the Soviet Union.

This is not accidental; Texas has more automobiles than any state except California — more than most sovereign nations — and Texans like to drive wherever they choose. In the 1930s there was a tremendous push to "get Texas out of the mud"; the elan (fostered by an imposing "highway lobby" that supports one of the largest expenditures of state government and one of the biggest industries in the state) has not ebbed in recent years.

CHARLES O'REAR

Soon after 1900 a new phase of development began. Most of the Great High Plains is not suitable for small farming, but with the appearance of heavy agricultural machinery, steam plows, the soil could be broken for huge fields. Wheat and cotton planting were started on a large scale. The first wave of settlers were cattlemen; now a second stream came out of Kansas and the Middle West to farm the land. The Panhandle quickly turned into one of the largest wheat-raising sections of the nation.

Finally, about the middle of the century, the vast ground water reserves of the Ogallala Formation began to be pumped up for irrigation. These, combined with chemical fertilizers, turned millions of acres of pasture into green fields.

The sea of grass is gone now, but big farms and big ranches still spread out over the big land under the big sky. Roads cross the landscape everywhere. And everywhere, it seems, civilization has made a mark. But the small Panhandle towns for all their neat modernity still seem to sit precariously on the plowed curvature of earth beneath that sky. Man has carved the earth to his will, but he is still a mere speck upon the land. •

Heart-shaped cemetery at Booker: The town of Booker (1,219) is situated in ranch country in the far northeast corner of the Panhandle. It has an unusual history, being one of the few towns that was ever physically moved, building by building and piece by piece, across a state line. Booker was La Kemp, Oklahoma, until 1919, when the Panhandle and Santa Fe Railroad extended a line from Shattuck, Oklahoma, into Texas. To put the settlement on the rail line, the inhabitants simply moved it into Texas, renaming the town Booker after a railroad civil engineer. In today's bureaucratic society, such an event would probably be impossible, if not illegal; things were freer on the frontier.

Like many cities in the region Booker, although a small place, lies in two counties. County lines were drawn as arbitrary squares or rectangles on the map by the Texas Legislature when the plains were still Comanche country, without regard to terrain or how settlement might take place. Part of Booker is in Ochiltree, part in Lipscomb County.

Many people have come and gone on the High Plains; some went back East in defeat, some were driven on to California by drought and dust. But some families survived upon the land, and more rest eternally beneath it.

Panhandle fields: Very large farms, with extremely long plowed rows, are characteristic of the High Plains. Plantings from 5,000 to 10,000 acres are common and field rows often run for more than a mile.

The principal row crops are grain sorghum and cotton, which is farmed both dry land and with irrigation. The two are regularly planted together, with double rows of cotton interspersed with a row of grain. Maturing earlier, the grain serves as a wind break.

Strong winds sweep over this vast, high expanse, and during plowing season or dry spells, create severe dust storms. It sometimes seems to outsiders that the entire country must blow away; native landowners joke that after a good blow they have to meet and sort out whose fields are where.

But despite wind, drought, and the ever-present danger of untimely frost in both spring and fall, High Plains farmers produce huge harvests because of vast economies of scale.

CHARLES O'REAR

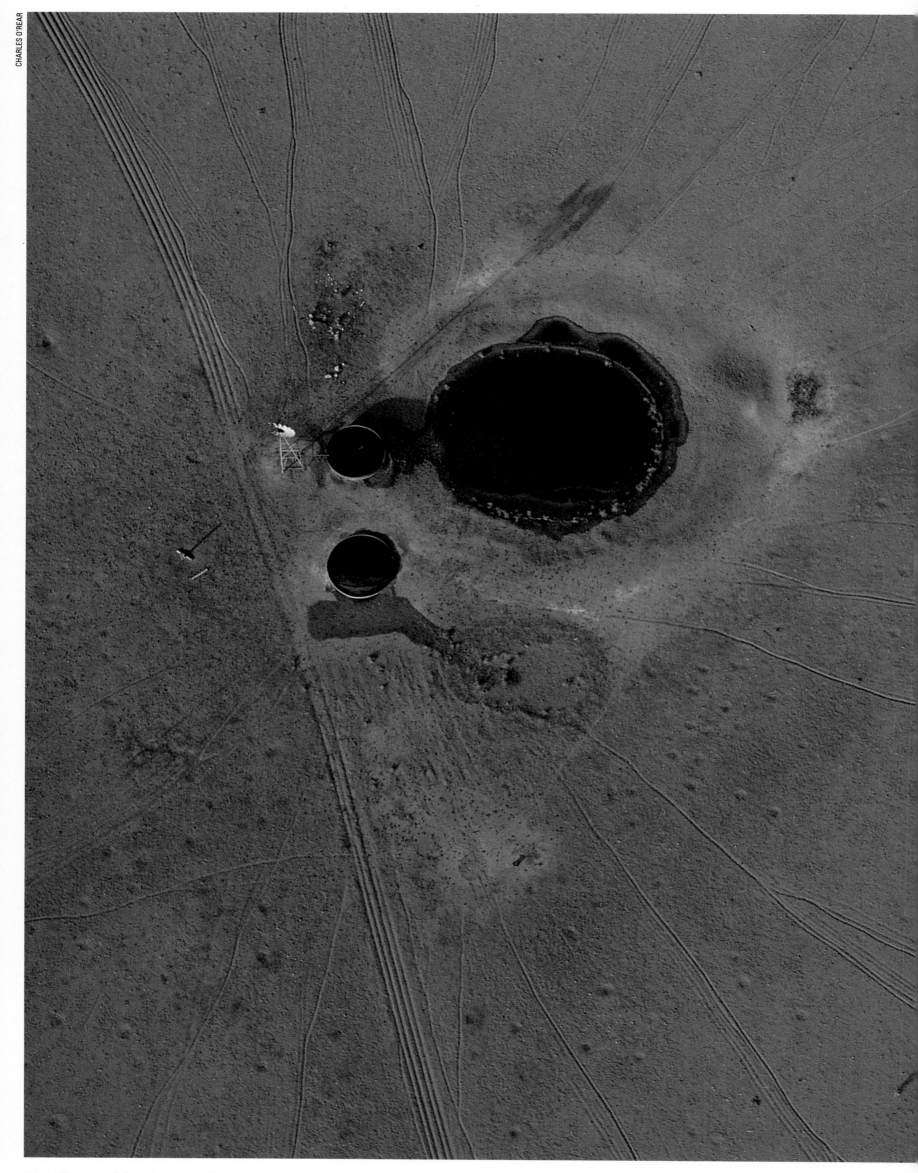

Water hole near Dumas: In the Panhandle, and in fact across most of Texas, there are not enough natural sources of water. The few streams are often unfit to drink, and the shallow natural lakes dry up in summer and fall. Through most of Texas, cattle are watered in "tanks" that are usually created by excavating an artificial pond to catch run-off from rains. On the High Plains, however, watering holes are usually low spots in a fold of ground, with or without a berm or levee. They normally depend on pumped water for a dependable supply.

The town of Dumas (12,194) is a thriving agribusiness and petroleum center, the seat of Moore County north of Amarillo. It has achieved a certain fame in another way: Phil Baxter of Navarro County once had to lay over here on his way to Denver. Struck by inspiration, he composed the song "Ding Dong Daddy from Dumas," later popularized by Phil Harris and known by millions of Americans who never had the faintest idea there was a Dumas or where it was.

CHARLES O'REAR

Sunset on Lake Meredith: There are few natural lakes in Texas, and virtually none on the High Plains. Lake Meredith was created between 1962-5 by damming the Canadian River by the Bureau of Reclamation. The fill extends from the southeastern corner of Hutchinson County through the southeastern quarter of Moore County and into Potter, near Amarillo. With a surface area of 21,640 acres and a storage capacity of 1,407,600 acre feet, Lake Meredith supplies water not only to Amarillo but to communities all across the Panhandle.

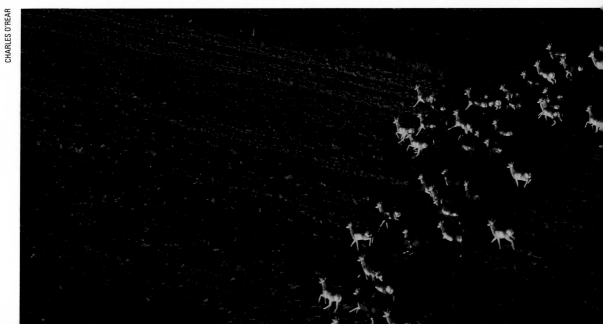

A herd of antelope near Buffalo Springs: The Panhandle, like most of Texas, once was a vast natural game preserve. In addition to the millions of buffalo, there were large numbers of antelope and deer, as well as smaller game and predators. The Comanches were always few in number and hardly made a dent on the wildlife population. White settlement and the development of large-scale ranching and farming changed all that. The buffalo, disliked by cattlemen both because the animals supported the Indians and competed with cattle for the range, were soon killed off by the hide hunters. One early settler, Charles Goodnight, however, foresaw the extinction of the bison (a few survived in Canada), and he preserved a small herd on his large ranch. These few animals were the progenitors of the rather numerous herds of "tame" buffalo now found in Texas and nearby states.

In more modern times a different spirit has moved many Texas landowners. Tax laws encourage preserving game areas, and wildlife is seen both as an economic boon — hunting is big business — and as a natural aesthetic asset.

Amarillo: Amarillo is the commercial heart and
only metropolis of the Panhandle. As such, it
serves not only the region but a broader area
that includes portions of five states. The hub of
a large oil and ranching empire, it is the
marketing and distributing center for the Texas
and Oklahoma Panhandles, northern New
Mexico, southern Colorado, and western
Kansas. Important industries include copper
refining, manufacturing, feedlot operations
and, of course, support functions for
agribusiness and petroleum production.
Amarillo is on the Randall-Potter County line;
it is the seat of Potter County but also provides
two-thirds of the population of Randall County
to the south. The city began in 1887 as
Ragtown, a collection of hide huts and tents
where Fort Worth and Denver Railroad hands
camped during construction. There were
competing settlements nearby, but Amarillo
absorbed or dominated them all and within a
few years emerged as one of the largest cattle-
shipping points in the world.
The name comes from a shallow lake nearby,
which Mexican herders called Amarillo (yellow)
because of the color of its banks.
When cotton, wheat, and feed crops began to
be produced in the Panhandle soon after 1900,
the growth of the city was assured.

Fields north of White Deer: Today a perfect picture of a prosperous agricultural area, the community of White Deer (population 1,210) had much the usual beginnings of Panhandle settlements. The country was named for a legendary white deer that frequented White Deer Creek. First enclosed in the White Deer (brand, Diamond F) Ranch in the 1880s, when the Panhandle and Santa Fe Railroad came through in 1887, the ranch sold off town lots and secured a post office. Some of the older, rougher breed of pioneer cattlemen hated settlers, wire, and development; the more far-seeing profited from them all.

The early years of the township were hard. Aside from ranching the only economic activity was gathering and selling bison bones. After hunters slaughtered the southern herds in the 1870s and early 1880s, millions of buffalo skeletons lay bleaching on the plains. For some years these could be sold to the railroad, which shipped them off to Kansas and other places to be ground up for fertilizer.

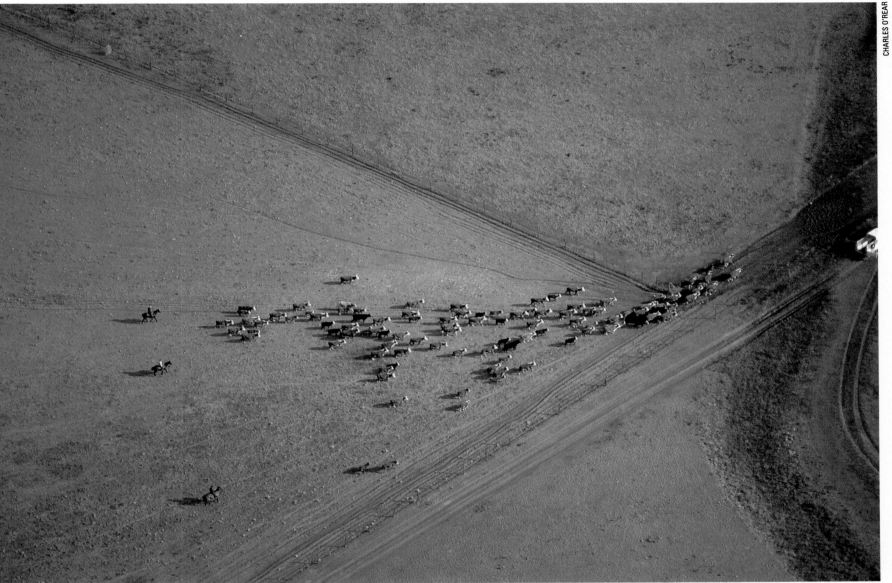

Cattle drive north of Pampa: Cattle drives are
no longer what they used to be. Once drovers
pushed vast herds for a thousand miles,
crossing the Canadian and Red Rivers on the
way to railheads in Kansas or to populate the
ranges of Wyoming and Montana. Now it's a
matter of moving cattle to a close-by shipping
point or to another pasture.

Pampa itself is an oil and cattle center, the seat
of Gray County northeast of Amarillo. It was
established by the Santa Fe Railroad in 1888
and named for the Spanish *pampas* — savannah
or plains — by someone who likened the
country to the vast pampas of the Argentine.

Right National Auto Salvage lot, Pampa: The National Auto Salvage company is owned by Dennis Caldwell, who operates two enormous salvage lots stacked with thousands of worn-out vehicles at any given time. The lot in Amarillo covers a mere 16 acres; this one at Pampa contains 97 acres of salvaged cars. This may not be the biggest salvage yard in the nation — but none, surely, is more spread out or more spectacular from the air.

Celanese plant southwest of Pampa: Manufacturing is now big business in Texas, although aside from making various sorts of machinery, it is overwhelmingly devoted to refining or processing mineral products of the Texas soil. Texas has the largest deposits of mineral and chemical earths in the nation, and from such mines come many things besides natural gas and crude oil. Although primarily located on the Gulf Coast, refining and petroleum product plants can be found wherever there is oil — and such activities have made Pampa, with its population of more than 20,000, more than a mere ranching town.

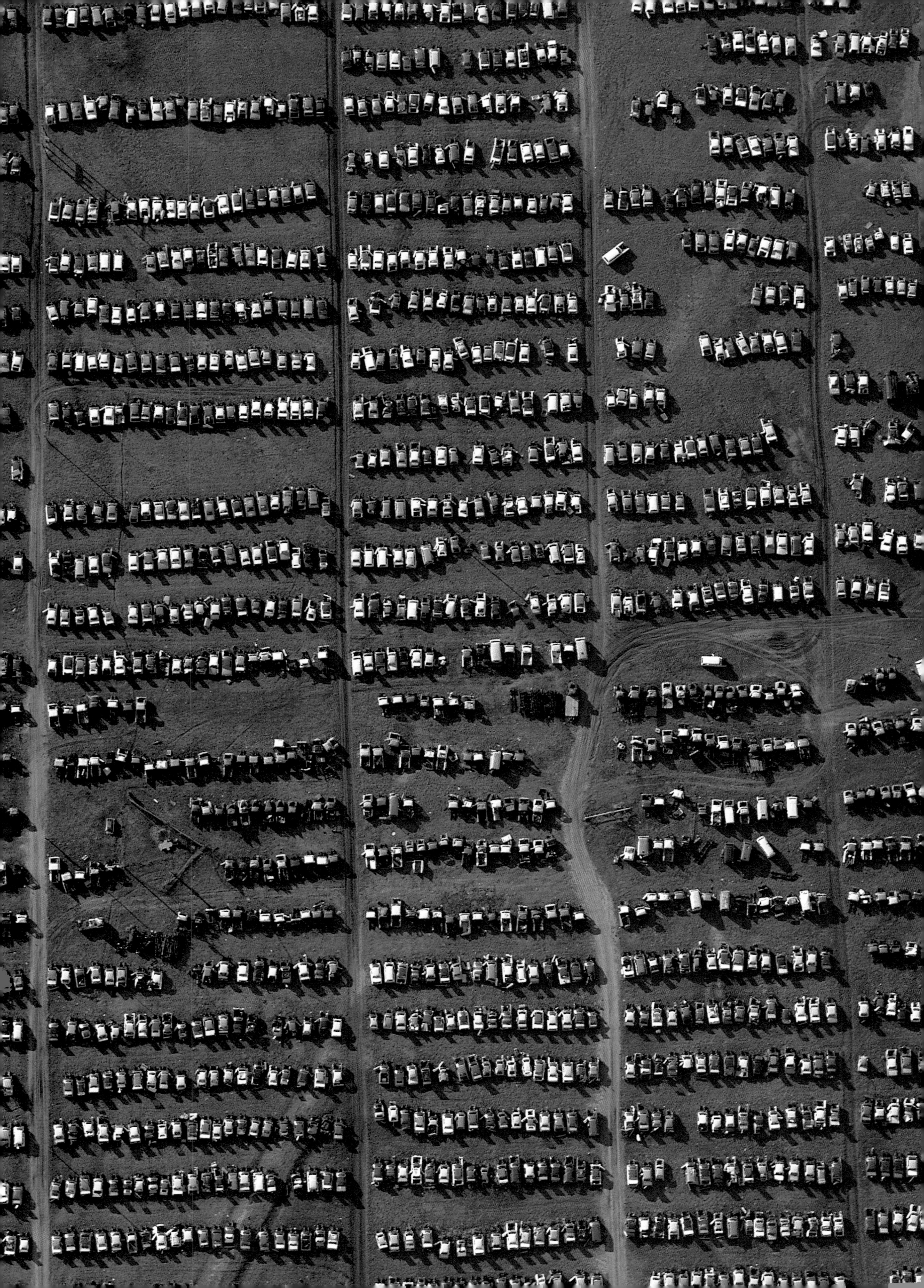

Cattle feed near Claude, Armstrong County: The great ranch of Armstrong County is the JA, southeast of Claude, in the Palo Duro Canyon at the foot of the Cap Rock Escarpment. Pioneer Texas trail driver and cattleman Charles Goodnight was the first to understand that the Comanche threat had been ended by the battle of Palo Duro Canyon in 1874 and that the High Plains was open for the taking. In 1876 he drove 1,600 head down from Colorado, choosing a ranch site in the canyon. Returning to get his wife — the country now seemed safe — he fell in with an English investor, John G. Adair, who agreed to finance a vast cattle operation on shares. Goodnight received one-third for managing.

The partnership, lasting ten years, built one of the finest ranches in the West. Afterward Goodnight purchased a portion of the JA— from Adair's initials — outright and began Quitaque Ranch near the present town that bears his name.

Some of the buildings Goodnight constructed in the 1880s still stand on the JA. The present main ranch house incorporates the original log cabin headquarters. The JA once sprawled over an immense empire: 580,000 acres owned and another 1.3 million leased by 1903. The ranch is smaller now, but it is still owned by descendants of John Adair.

In 1981 the JA was managed by Monte Richie, a grandson, then past 80 but still a working cowman.

Goodnight chose well from the pick of Comanche territory. The JA is considered perhaps the most ideal of the great West Texas spreads. It is watered well by the Red River; the canyon provides protected winter range; and the surrounding plains are among the best grasslands on the High Plains.

Left Oil field near Kellerville: The Arab oil embargo and OPEC price increases of the 1970s were an ill wind that blew Texas much good. In addition to the frenetic new drilling activity that convulsed West Texas and, to some degree, most of the state, many older oil fields were given a hard second look. Wells unprofitable with petroleum selling at $3 per barrel became bonanzas when the price reached $30 and more. All this created new activity in the Panhandle and across the South Plains, regions with great reserves of oil — though without the fabulous concentrations found in the Permian Basin.

Pulling units are used to work over existing producing wells. They are often mistaken for drilling rigs; the actual units are similar and can be converted to each use. However, a true drilling rig is surrounded by the signs of raw earth and activity, mud pits and storage units. Pulling units lack the above-ground rig, with rotary table and kelly underneath.

Above Field south of Claude: While the Panhandle as a whole is a high, seemingly endless plain, the ground in most places is far from level. It rolls and undulates and, once broken by the plow, is subject to enormous wind and water erosion. Countless tons of this earth have been carried away over the years. To hold down the damage, various forms of contour plowing are employed, with ridges to prevent widespread erosion. Claude, though primarily noted for the fine ranching country in the vicinity, has farming too. The seat of Armstrong County, it lies north of Palo Duro Canyon and the Prairie Dog Town Fork of the Red River. Claude was the name of the locomotive engineer who brought the first train here when the settlement was end o' track for the Fort Worth and Denver Railroad in 1887. The downtown, incidentally, was the location for the film "Hud," made from Larry McMurty's novel, *Horseman, Pass By*.

Red soil fields southwest of Shamrock: Red
and brown soils are found in Texas principally
on the Llano Estacado and Edwards Plateau,
but some are on the rolling North Central
Plains, as here near Shamrock, a town of 2,834
on the eastern edge of the Panhandle.
Reddish color usually indicates soils formed by
freshwater sources such as rivers or lakes; red
soils are often found in the flood deltas of West
Texas near the confluence of rivers and
streams. In some places the reddish-brown
soils become red sands. Red sands are
normally created by iron, the agent used by
living things to fix oxygen from the air.
In Texas, red soils are often associated with
white soils and caliche rock, which are ocean-
created layers of earth over which the
freshwater red soils have been deposited as
the fresh water moved seaward.
Some such soils are inorganic. The time of
their formation was the Middle Precambrian
period, about one billion years ago. One of the
forms of this inorganic stone is hematite, used
by the Plains Indians to make paint, and
probably their favorite pigment.
Red soils are considered as good as black soils
for farming; however, in most areas where red
soils occur ranching tends to be the major
activity, not because of the quality of the earth
but because of the lack of rainfall. These
agriculture areas usually require irrigation, and
red soils also need nitrogen fertilizers because
of low nitrogen content.
Where orange-colored soils appear, it is often
more a trick of light than the true color of the
earth.

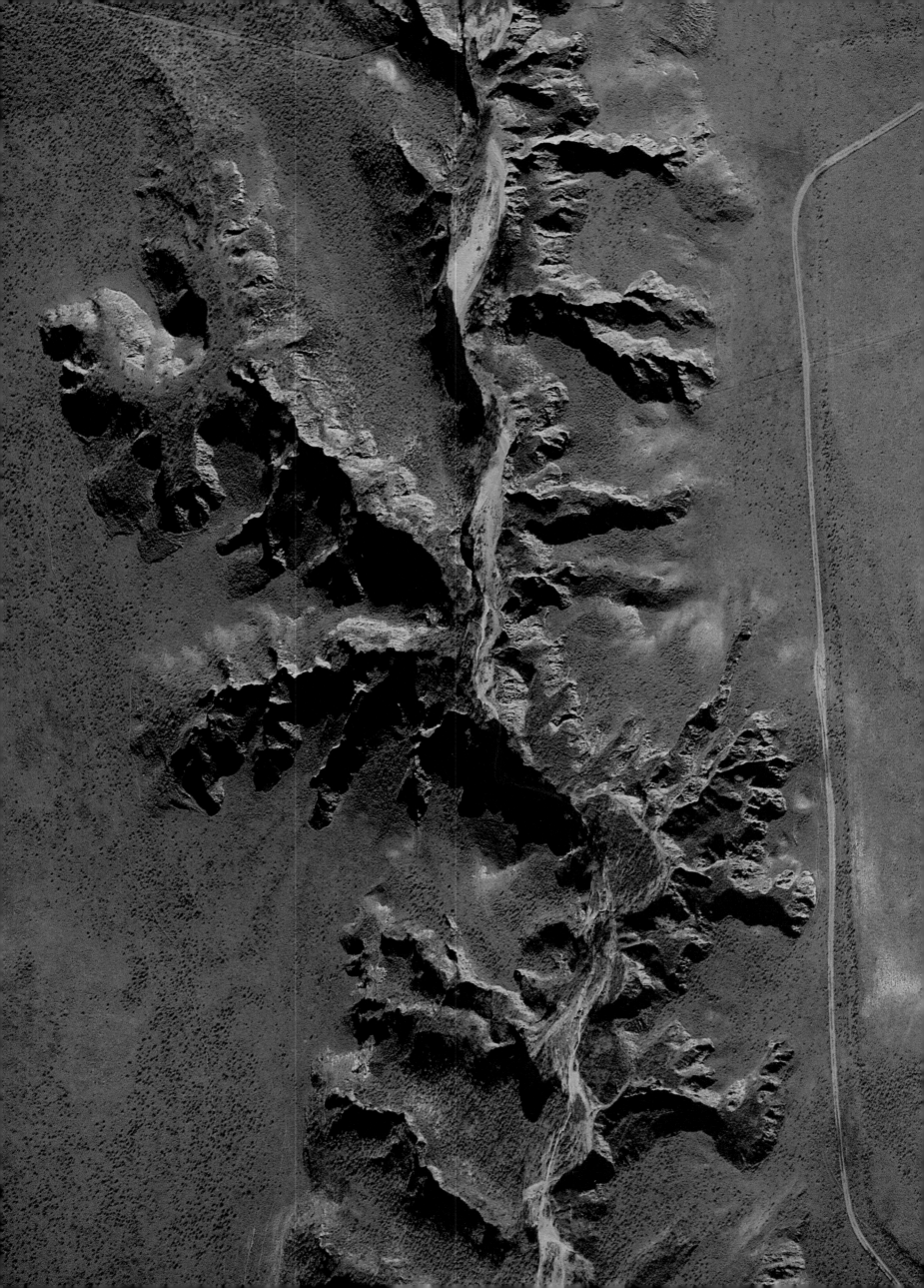

Left   Orange soils near Shamrock.

Above   Downtown Wellington: Wellington, population 3,000, is the seat of Collingsworth County in the southeastern corner of the Panhandle near the Oklahoma line. And behind this fact lies an interesting history.

The site of present Wellington was on the land of the old Rocking Chair Ranch. When the countryside seemed sufficiently populated and civilized to organize a county, in 1890 the small settlement of Pearl some two miles north seemed likely to be designated the seat of county government. But this was always a matter of vast local importance in the developing West — the courthouse brought both prestige, business, and improved land values. On election day the Rocking Chair foreman told all his hands to vote for Wellington, named for the victor of Waterloo. Later, Wellington and Collingsworth County almost started another War Between the States. In 1860, the Texas Legislature had created a Greer County, which included not only present Collingsworth and Wheeler Counties but also part of the Indian Territory of Oklahoma. In 1886, when Texans tried to organize this county, they became involved in a dispute with the United States government. This was finally resolved by the Supreme Court in 1906, which fixed the present boundary between the two states.

Palo Duro Canyon: The Palo Duro, which lies southeast of Amarillo in Randall County, is a spectacular canyon cut through the rock by millennia of water action by the Prairie Dog Fork of the Red River as it emerges from the Llano Estacado into the rolling plains of the eastern Panhandle.

Palo Duro Canyon was the site of one of the most decisive, though almost bloodless, battles of the Indian wars. Unknown to Texans or the Army, it was the hidden fortress of Quanah, war chief of the Kwahadi Comanches. Col. Ranald S. Mackenzie, commanding the 4th Cavalry, had pursued the Comanches across West Texas for years; he rarely found the Indians — but they found him when they wanted, with lightning descents on horseback to kill troopers and steal horses, forcing the infantry to fight from barricaded wagons. After a frustrating campaign that began in 1872, Mackenzie determined that the Comanches must have a great, secret camp somewhere in the unmapped vastness of the Panhandle.

In 1874, after an Indian uprising that carried fire and blood to the corners of five states, Mackenzie led the Southern Column as part of a large, integrated maneuver of Army forces out of Fort Concho toward the Llano Estacado. Mackenzie was not an Indian-hater but a professional soldier, and the best Indian-fighter in the West. He devised, in Texas, the search-and-destroy tactics that were later used by Miles and Crook (and most stupidly by Custer) in all the latter-day campaigns. He knew that the Indians traveled with their women and children, and to defeat them and drive them to the Indian Territory reservations he had to find and destroy their camp.

The records of the Southern Column do not tell the whole story. Mackenzie seized a Comanchero, one of the part-Indian New Mexican traders who sold guns to the Comanches in exchange for captives and stolen cattle, and by brutal methods made him give away Quanah's hiding place, known then only to the Comancheros.

On September 27, Sergeant Charlton and two Tonkawa scouts discovered the lip of the canyon. They crawled on their hands and knees to the edge. Far below, they saw hundreds of ponies grazing on the canyon floor and tepees strung out along the river for three miles — a vast encampment of Comanches and allied Kiowas and Cheyennes.

Mackenzie had found his Indians. But he was no Custer. He dropped his supply train and marched his whole command, 600 men, all night to reach Palo Duro. Then at dawn, scouts leading, he sent the troopers down over a rough trail on which the men could only go in single file, leading their horses.

Company after company reached the canyon meadow, but before they could form in line the camp was aroused. Mackenzie ordered A Company to stampede the Indians' horse herd. In a desperate race, the cavalry arrived first, driving off the whole *caballado*.

On foot, unable to mount and fight in their accustomed manner, the Indians set up a covering fire and retreated up the canyon, following their women and children. Mackenzie did not attack or pursue; he was also no Chivington. He did not need to.

He had seized 1,400 horses, almost every horse the Indians had, and almost all their food and ammunition. Knowing that the Comanches would try to retake the unmanageable horse herd, he ordered it destroyed at the mouth of Tule Canyon. In this slaughter, which sickened the troopers, there was more firing and more blood than in the "battle." Only one Indian was killed and an Army trumpeter wounded.

But this blow destroyed forever the power of the Indians on the southern plains. Without horses, the warriors could neither hunt nor fight. The Army swept up starving bands over the winter, and the next year Quanah surrendered the remnants of the Comanches at Fort Sill in the Indian Territory.

Outside Texas, which had lived with Comanche terror for two generations, Mackenzie's victory was little noticed or understood. The fiasco at the Little Big Horn drew more notice. As Sergeant Charlton wrote, the blue-clad troopers had gone down into the jaws of death in a very risky operation, fought a winning fight without massacre, but rode back unheralded. Now, on summer nights at Palo Duro Canyon State Park near Amarillo, these events and the struggles of the pioneers are remembered in a sound and light show, the musical "Texas," which has become one of the most popular tourist attractions in the state.

Overleaf
Palo Duro Canyon.

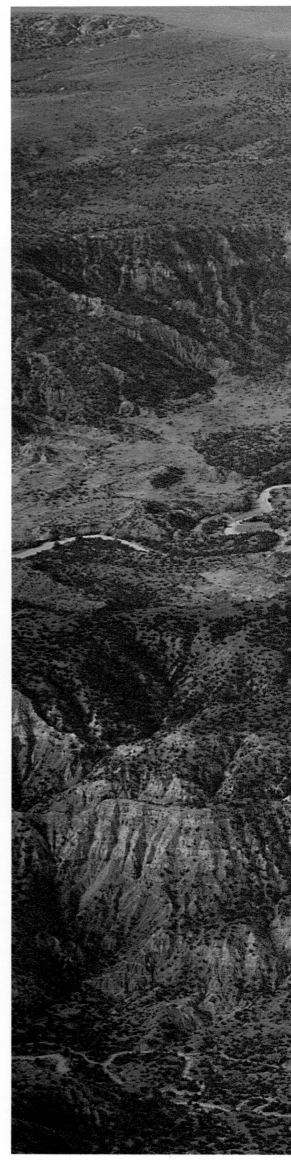

Left Plowed fields near Turkey.

Right Turkey, Texas: There is a Turkey, Texas, although many Americans probably believe the name is an invention of television scriptwriters.

Turkey is just below and east of the Llano Estacado in Hall County west of Childress. The town, population 644, got its name from wild turkeys that used to roost along Turkey Creek, named for the same reason. It was first known as Turkey Roost, but when the community received a post office in 1893, the name was shortened and dignified.

The rails only reached Turkey in 1928, but this caused the building of a large hotel and other trappings of civilization. The wild turkeys are gone, but Turkey lives, surrounded by plowed fields — a pleasant, peaceful town on the Rolling Plains.

There is a marker in Turkey commemorating the late, great country musician Bob Wills. Wills was raised here, and he worked as a barber, playing at country dances at night. He led the Lightcrust Doughboys and the Texas Playboys bands and wrote "San Antonio Rose" and other country-western classics.

Turkey

Red rocks between Turkey and Parnell, Hall County.

Right Cotton bales, Turkey: Cotton is no longer king in Texas, as it was before the Civil War and long after. But it is still big business, one of the most important products of the state.

Since 1880, Texas has led all the states in cotton production, and it normally accounts for more than one-third the total U.S. production. Annual yields during the past 10 years have ranged from 2.5 million to 5.5 million bales, averaging almost 4 million bales per annum. The amount varies not only because of weather and harvests but because of national agricultural policy. In some years farmers are paid, by one means or another, to grow cotton; in others, support prices, acreage limitations and the like are changed by Congress.

The value of cotton lint averaged more than $1 billion between 1979-1981, but fell to $678 million in 1982, largely because of reduced acreage. In a typical year, between 4 million-8 million acres will be planted. The vast majority of this acreage is in Upland cotton, a much smaller amount in American Pima.

Texas cotton is almost exclusively machine-planted, cultivated (though chopping or thinning is done by hand) and harvested. Much of the ginned and baled crop seen here is destined for foreign markets.

CHARLES O'REAR

Boxcars on a siding near Quitaque: Old Charles
Goodnight, who ended up near here after
driving cattle over half the Southwest, never
saw such a sight — but the lonely sidings of
West Texas rails are regularly lined with miles
of empty boxcars.

This is a convenient place to store unused cars
between peak seasons. In winter, especially,
thousands may be pushed onto sidings to await
the rush times of harvest.

CHARLES O'REAR

Overleaf

Empty cotton trailers waiting for picking time: Like rail boxcars, cotton trailers — used to haul cotton from the fields to gins — spend much of their time waiting. The roads are jammed with them during the fall picking, and no matter how fast the turn-around time between field and gin, there never seems to be enough of them. But for about ten months of the year they remain, either in some yard beside a gin or in a farmer's compound. Each summer they have to be made ready for the harvest; this frequently involves a bit of fix-up, re-tiring, painting, and hammering.

In recent years, methods have been developed to compress picked cotton bolls in the field, given the impossibility of hauling a large crop to limited gin capacity. The cotton is formed into a sort of bale or module and left beside the fields, sometimes in the early snows of fall or winter. Protected in this way from the elements or from simply blowing away, it may be taken for ginning at leisure.

The Cap Rock Escarpment: The Cap Rock is the outstanding terrain feature of the Panhandle, separating the Llano Estacado on the west from the Rolling Plains. From Coronado, the first Spanish explorer of these parts, to the latest tourist in his air-conditioned automobile, the traveler has always been startled when he first sees it.

The break in the landscape is dramatic. Up on the escarpment the land is an eternity of flatness, a treeless plain that seems to go on endlessly. Even the rivers that cross this expanse are hidden beneath the surface of the land: over millions of years they have cut deep, narrow canyons. The transition, or fall-off, comes within the span of a man's arm. The Llano Estacado ends (or begins) abruptly, rising 200 feet, 500 feet, and in some places as much as 1,000 feet from the rolling countryside below. From the lip, looking east, the vista spreads out for 40 miles of rolling fields and pastures, dips and hollows, with scrub oak thickets along winding rivers.

The Cap Rock is actually a sort of geologic rubble heap. The rocks and other material are a generally uniform mix that eroded from the Rockies to the west. Because these materials are so hard, they did not erode as quickly as the softer rocks and soils to the east. They thrust upward where the softer soils begin like the walls of some god's castle. While the entire escarpment runs, roughly, from Big Spring far to the south to Amarillo, it is most distinctive and visible in Borden County and the area east of Lubbock.

The Cap Rock is a highly mineral rock created as water erosion carried minerals from the top of the layer to the bottom under great pressure. This process caused a very hard formation — a "hard pan" — through which water cannot penetrate. This hard pan underlies the entire Llano. It is the reason for its flatness.

Above the hard-pan rock are the red soils and sands of the High Plains. When it rains here, the water seeps through these soils, continuing the Cap Rock formation, until it meets the hard level underneath. Here it collects in vast pools or aquifers while slowly seeking a path downward to the sea. The springs and seeps on the Edwards Plateau far to the southeast are the outlets for these aquifers, but meanwhile they provide the ground water that makes the irrigated portions of the High Plains bloom.

Controversy still swirls over the original meaning of the Spanish name Llano Estacado, given the High Plains by Coronado in the 1540s. One theory holds that because these plains were so trackless and devoid of terrain features, the Spaniards staked out their return route — thus, "Staked Plains." The other argument is that the Spanish *estacado* also means "palisaded," and that Coronado meant to call them the Palisaded Plains. The key is probably that Coronado was a soldier and saw the sharp, abrupt thrust of the Cap Rock as resembling a military palisade, the stakes used for fortifications.

When seen from the east, and especially from the Pecos River Valley to the west (from which Coronado's expedition approached), the Cap Rock looks very much like the walls of a fortified place. From the Texas side, however, the view is more spectacular. More can be seen; the elevation from the plain is greater; the escarpment seems longer. The argument goes on, and the choice comes down to historians' prejudices in the matter.

The streams that cut through the Cap Rock on their way to the sea emerge from the escarpment through the great Palo Duro and Tule Canyons. These canyons have been formed exactly like the Grand Canyon farther west on the other side of the Continental Divide. Given millions more years of such action, they will become as deep and spectacular as the canyons of the Colorado River.

Overleaf
The Cap Rock Escarpment.

Snow-covered fields near Happy, Swisher County: Snowfall plays a major role in both the ecology and economy of the Panhandle. It provides a significant source of moisture, and nurtures and protects the winter wheat that is planted extensively in the region. Planting is done before the first big winter snows, and harvesting takes place in late spring or early summer; the wheat crop is usually out sometime in July.

The configuration of the land from place to place determines the amount of snowfall. Where snows are good, the wheat grows best. In fact, a lack of winter snows can be disastrous to the Panhandle.

Wheat replaced the native buffalo grass soon after the turn of the century when the rails brought farmers into the former ranch lands. While many small farmers came at first — and some remain — the vicissitudes of drought, disastrous commodity prices, and dust bowls over the years have caused the creation of larger and larger farming operations. Yields are relatively low in Texas; this requires more planting, and larger plantings demand more land and capital, credit and machinery.

Texas ranked fifth in wheat production in 1982, third in 1981; wheat is normally the second most valuable crop after cotton. Texas farmers plant some 8 million acres per year, harvesting about 6 million. And since some wheat acres are grazed by cattle, these also appear in cattle statistics — which is why such figures are reported inexactly.

Left

Muleshoe, Texas: The name always intrigues outsiders, but the town of Muleshoe, population 4,842, seat of Bailey County in the southwestern corner of the Panhandle near the New Mexico line, has never had anything to do with mules. At least, it has had no more to do with mules than any other part of Texas in the days when mules were widely used.

The name was derived from the Muleshoe Ranch, whose brand was an inverted U over a bar — a muleshoe. The Ranch did not raise mules; the brand was one of convenience, like that of the XIT. However, the town humorously maintains a memorial to Army mules of World War 1.

Today the Muleshoe area is mainly devoted to a rich, irrigated agriculture.

Overleaf

Plowing near Muleshoe: The Muleshoe area boasts a more diversified agriculture than is found in most places across the Panhandle and South Plains. The soil is sandy and quite rich, and it holds moisture well. The ground is sufficiently level to encourage extensive irrigation. Summer also seems to linger late here. All this encourages the growing of a large variety of cash crops such as corn, potatoes, onions, beans, tomatoes and melons. Vegetable processing and shipping sheds stand beside the ubiquitous grain silos. Cotton, of course, is also planted. There are even some experiments with grapevines.

All forms of irrigation are used here: circular, sprinkler (from a great rig on wheels, drawn by tractor), and gravity flow. Texans are testing Israeli methods of drip irrigation, pioneered in the Negev Desert and successfully used in California. These use less precious water but are more useful with orchards and smaller plots in other parts of the state.

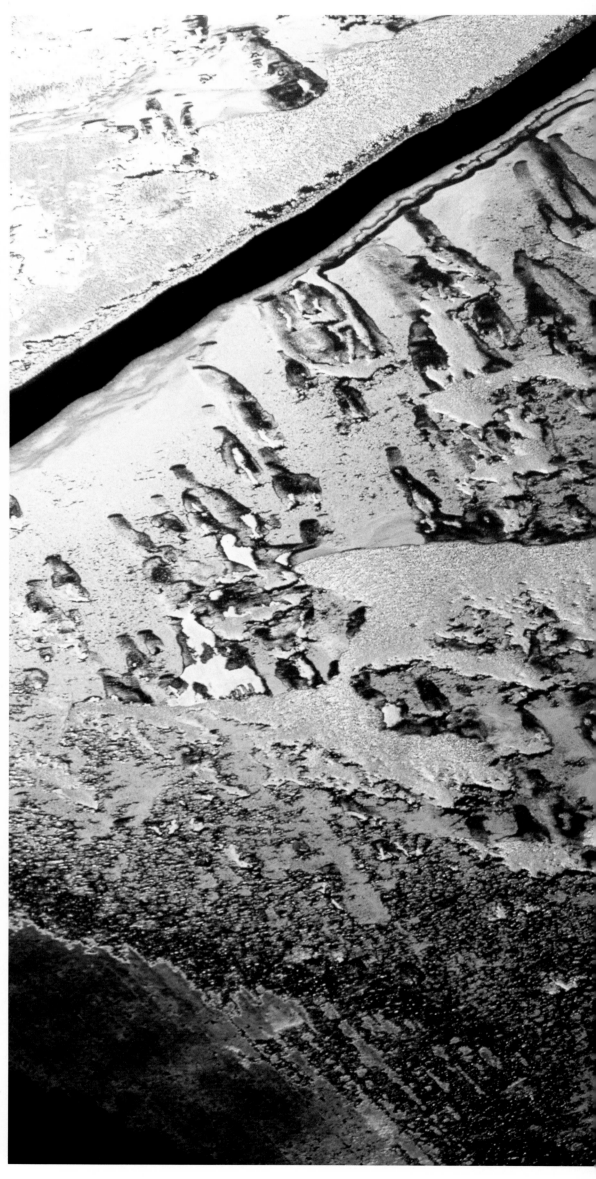

Winter near Conway, Carson County: Situated in the middle of the North American continent, nearly all of Texas is subject to extremes of weather. Summers are quite hot, with temperatures frequently cracking 100 degrees Fahrenheit; Arctic cold fronts whipping down the plains from Canada periodically cause severe freezes. Yet the High Plains records are not so extreme as in more sheltered spots. July mean temperatures are in the 90s, and January mean lows around 20 degrees, although during severe weather the mercury may drop to 10 or 20 degrees of frost. Snowfall is light but is beneficial in terms of moisture.

Over most of the Panhandle the first killing frost comes in October, and the last freeze of spring in April. This makes a growing season of 180 to 195 days.

THE PAN HANDLE ☆ 91

Wildorado: Wildorado is in the southeastern corner of Oldham County on Interstate Highway 40 and the Chicago, Rock Island and Pacific Railroad due west of Amarillo.

The area was first settled in the nineteenth century by ranchers Eugene Binford and J. R. Goodman. A settlement started in 1900 when the Chicago, Rock Island, and Gulf Railroad designated it as a cattle-shipping point. The name, like so many others in the Panhandle, was chosen by railroad employees. Whether they had in mind a potential El Dorado in the wilderness is unknown.

By 1915 Wildorado boasted a population of 100 and a post office. But it was eclipsed by Amarillo, only 13 miles away. The town is yet unincorporated, with only 180 inhabitants. Still, it has a dozen businesses rated by Dunn and Bradstreet.

Cattle feedlot near Wildorado: Feedlots are prominent along Interstate 40 in the environs of Amarillo, the movements of whose cattle feedlot market are watched across the nation. The range raises cattle, but this is where beef is made. A large feedlot looks like a city when lit up at night. Day or night, it can be distinguished downwind by the smell. Cattle (or sheep and lambs) are penned and fed continuously from bins with scientifically formulated diets to create the meat Americans prefer in steaks and hamburgers.

Right   Oil and agriculture blend near Whiteface in Cochran County on the southern fringes of the Panhandle: On the High Plains the big businesses of the region are inextricably mixed. Modern oil operations no longer significantly pollute land or water. Fields are plowed around pump jacks; cattle graze between them. A common sight is grain or cotton fields dotted with derricks or oil pumps, or cattle feeding on wheat stubble.
Texans can always tell the farmer or rancher who has oil wells on his place; he's always more independent, and sometimes even obnoxious. At any rate, happy is the landowner who combines all three.

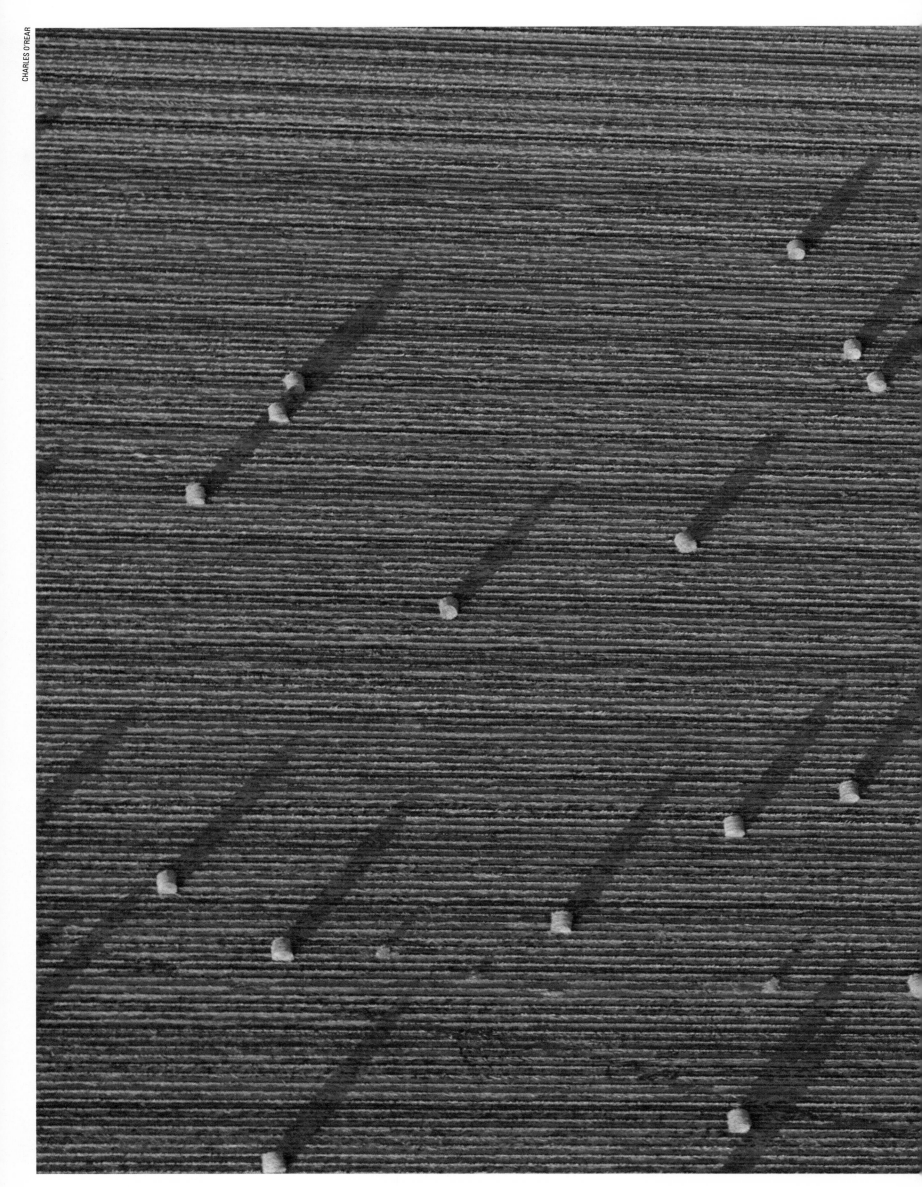

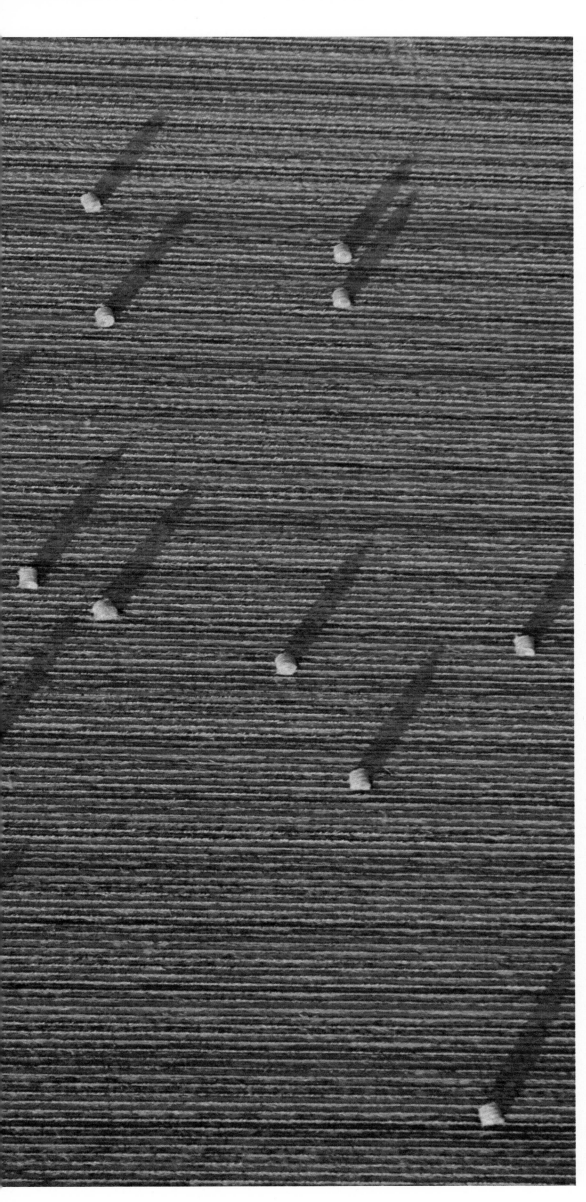

Baled hay near Petersburg, Hale County: Hay, of course, is an important crop in cattle country, and it is produced both for local use and for sale in other parts of Texas, especially during drought or periods when range cattle must be fed. The hay is cut and baled by machine, then fork-lifted onto trucks for transportation to its destination.

Nearby Petersburg was once in neighboring Floyd County; it consisted mainly of a post office run by and named for Mrs. Margaret Peters. In 1902, Ed White opened a general store where Petersburg now stands and drew the post office five miles west into Hale County. Although the town was plotted by 1909, it did not collect more than 100 inhabitants until the Fort Worth and Denver track was laid in 1928. The present population is 1,633.

Overleaf

Sheep grazing in plowed field near Floydada: Texas is mainly thought of as cattle country, but it also has great numbers of sheep and goats; Texas is the leading wool and slaughter lamb producer in the nation. However, the High Plains is not noted for sheep or wool production; most of this is centered to the south and east on the Edwards Plateau, where this constitutes the land's best use.

Floydada, the seat of Floyd County, is on the eastern edge of the Llano Estacado; the population is about 4,000. The residents wanted to name the settlement Floyd City, but this was opposed by the U.S. Post Office. Floydada came from the combination of Floyd and Ada, from Ada Price, member of a family that donated the land for the township.

Page 100-101

Field in Floyd County: Farming has come a long way in Texas since the days of impoverished sharecroppers and back-breaking labor under a burning sun. Farmers still go broke in plenty, and in season the workdays run from "can see to cain't see" — but on the High Plains nearly everything is now done by machines. In fact, farming is more properly called "agribusiness" in Texas; growers need to be adept mechanics and to keep abreast of all technological improvements in seed, fertilizers, irrigation; they need to understand credit and banking. Some read the *Wall Street Journal* for marketing and commodity price news.

Farming has been made profitable mainly because of huge economies in scale. Huge tractors drag multiple plows or cultivating blades, and one man can do the work in a day that once took a family weeks. The big tractors are usually diesel-powered; they have air-conditioned cabs with tape decks. Naturally, these are expensive, and the rising cost of equipment is a problem. Both for cost and convenience, contractors do much of the harvesting. Cotton, corn, and grain are planted by machine, tilled by machine, and harvested by a machine directly into trucks that will carry the produce to storage.

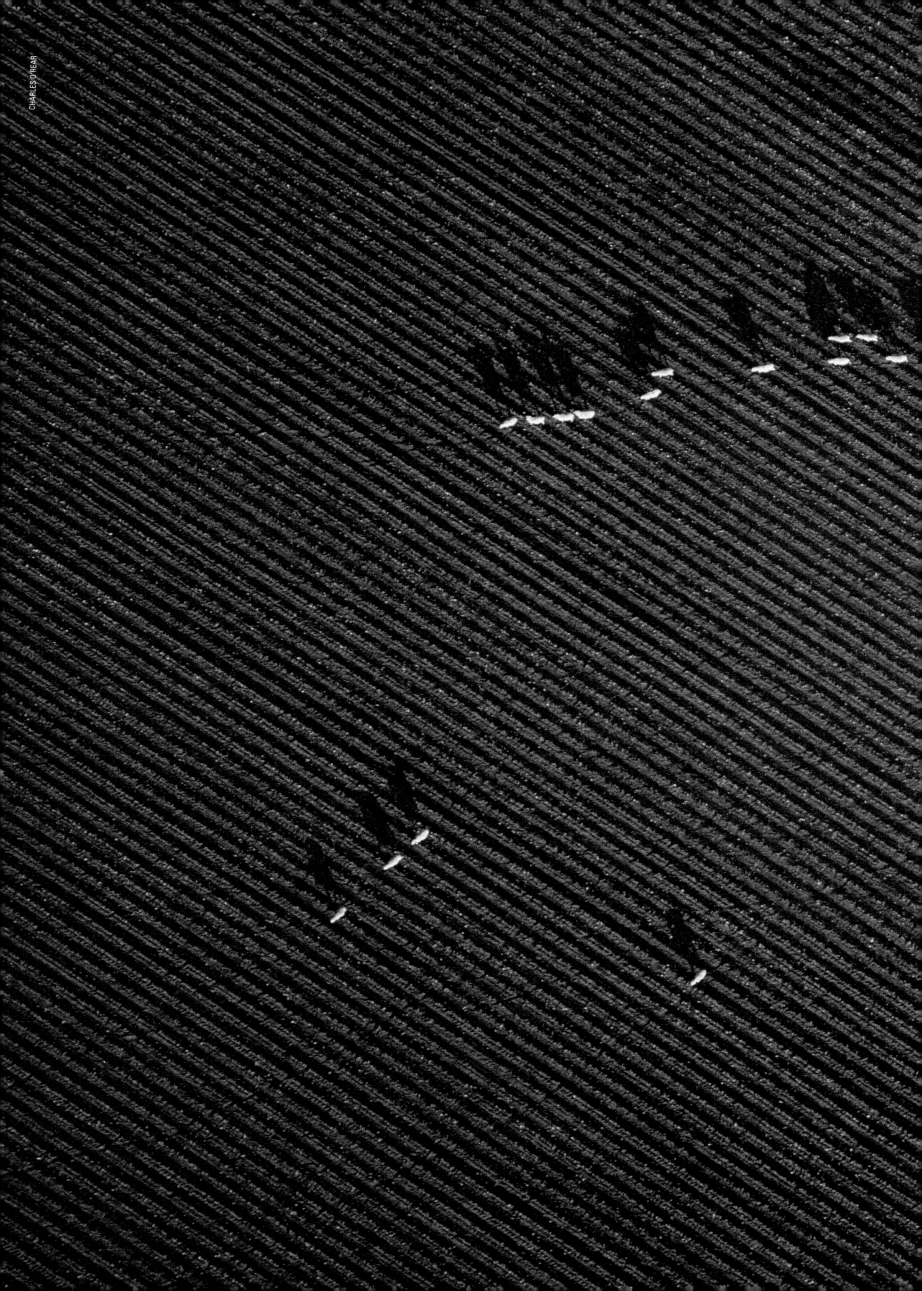

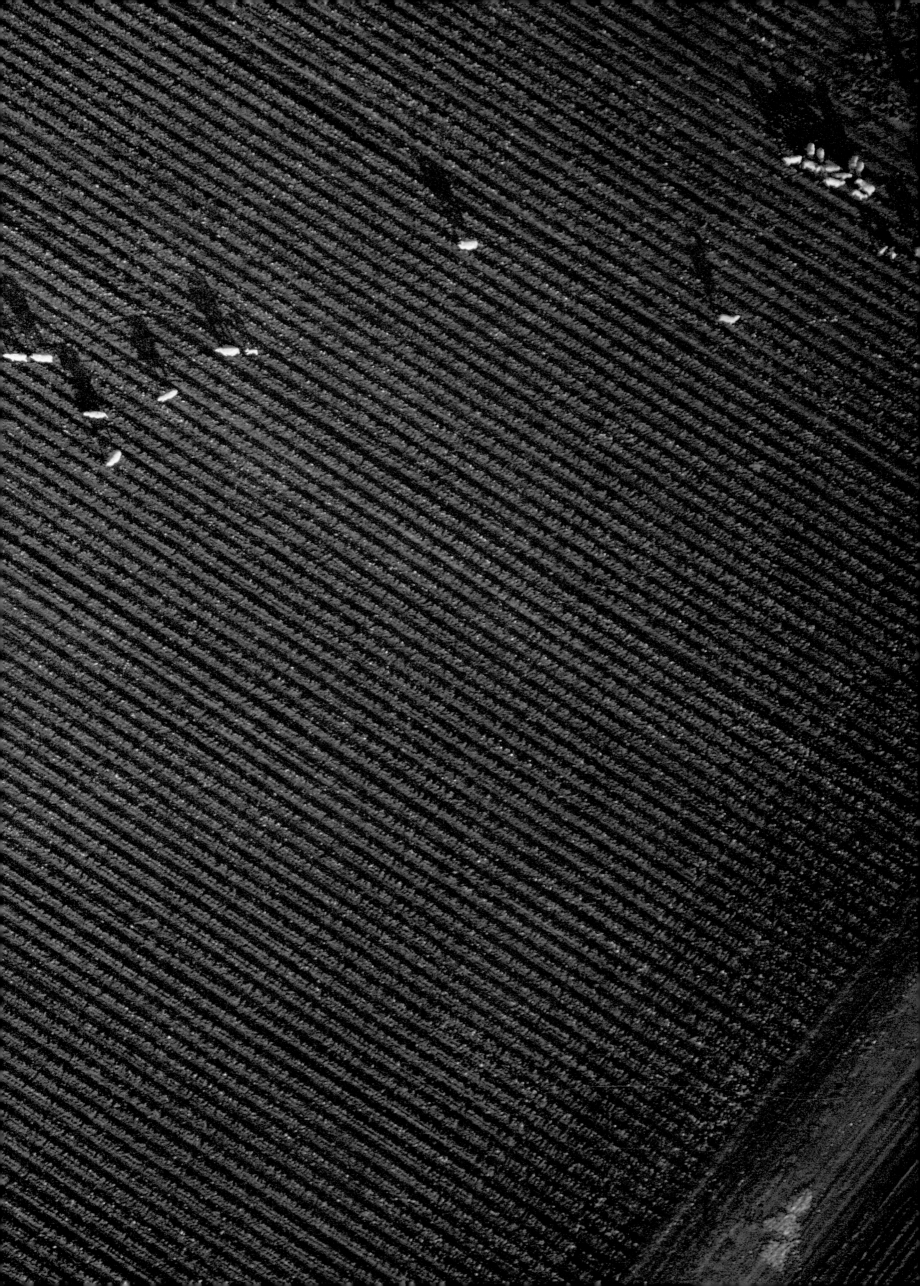

Ephemeral lakes on the South Plains, Lubbock County: The High Plains of Texas is marked with many shallow depressions. In winter and spring these low spots fill with water, becoming the so-called *playa* lakes. They normally evaporate, however, under the burning sun of summer. In the old days such lakes watered the millions of buffalo that wintered here, moving northward again in spring and summer.

West Texas

West Texas is a state of heart and mind. Geographically, however, it may be said to include all of Texas that falls west of the "rainfall line" separating the prairies and plains from the eastern timberlands. The line runs between the 98th and 100th meridians; west of this imaginary demarcation the rain falls less than 20–22 inches annually, not enough for trees or for non-irrigated agriculture. Drawn on the map, the line would extend from the Cross Timbers west of Fort Worth south through Abilene to Del Rio on the Rio Grande.

The whole of "West Texas" takes in both the Panhandle and the Trans-Pecos region; however, these are usually designated separately under those names. They are such special regions that they have been treated individually. Removing them still leaves West Texas a very big place, larger than most European nations.

The West Texas covered in this part includes the North Central Plains, a vast, rolling region where tallgrass prairies merge into short-grass savannahs, beginning at the Cross Timbers in the east and ending at the Cap Rock Escarpment in the west. It covers the South Plains and Edwards Plateau, which are the lower fringes of the North American Great Plains. This is the drainage area of the Colorado, Concho, San Saba, and Llano Rivers. It blends with the Llano Estacado and the North Central Plains to the north, and closes with the Balcones Escarpment in the south; the Colorado and the Pecos Rivers form its eastern and western boundaries.

The western regions together comprise about 40 percent of Texas' area but have a total population of about two million, some 15 percent of the people in the state. West Texas has all the least populated counties, and only one West Texas county (Lubbock) ranks among the top 20 in population.

The history of West Texas has been largely determined by the land and its aridity. While the land once supported millions of buffalo — without fences animals could range over the expanse for water and grass — only windmills, wire, and rails made this country accessible to stockmen. Later came farming and agribusiness, with the discovery of usable underground water and mechanization. Finally, there was oil, which from the 1920s became the dominant factor in many West Texas communities.

The economy now rests on three foundations: First, petroleum exploration and production in the Permian Basin, which includes most of West Texas and "Little West Texas" in eastern New Mexico. Midland and Odessa are the petroleum capitals of West Texas. The Permian Basin produces between 20–25 percent of all domestic oil and natural gas.

Second is ranching, including beef and milk cattle on the plains and far west, with sheep and goats on the Edwards Plateau. San Angelo is the largest primary wool market in the United States.

Finally, there is cotton and grain, raised wherever irrigation is possible, especially on the South Plains. Lubbock is the major cotton center in the state.

But the history and reality of West Texas were also made by its people. The majority of the pioneers were puritan Protestants, whether Southern Baptists, Methodists, or Church of Christ, or of other pentecostal groups. The culture and laws — for West Texas still abounds in "dry" counties where, by local option, alcoholic beverages may not be sold — reflect this heritage. But there is increasing awareness of the Mexican, Catholic, and Jewish heritages, which are extensive. In the case of the Hispanic, the heritage goes back to the explorations of Coronado.

Because of the ongoing struggle to master this land and the closeness in time to the frontier, the independent frontier ethic still thrives in this part of Texas. It may be stronger here than in any place in the United States. The reason is simple: even now a person who is not independent, self-reliant, and industrious has a hard time in West Texas. The country forges an outlook and ethic that is more individualistic and atomistic than social or communal. The towns are mostly small; there is no anonymity. The distances are vast; the land is inescapable. The tests of nature are extreme: heat and cold; drought and flood; tornadic winds; sandstorms that choke the throat and blot the sun; plagues of insects; temperatures that pass 100 degrees Fahrenheit in summer under cloudless skies but plunge below zero in winter.

But at the same time the land holds a harsh, haunting loveliness. When the rains come slowly in spring and nights are mild during calving and lambing time — or when the residue of incredibly ancient sea life is found beneath one's acres — there is almost unimaginable bounty. Nature can be very good, as well as punishing. But nature and the land are never far from any West Texan's consciousness. If his own livelihood does not come directly from the soil, he still depends upon others whose fortunes are tied to the land.

With all this, and perhaps because of all this, opportunity remains as enormous as a West Texas sky. The land tests men and women, breaks them or makes them. Their mettle is revealed. And for this reason the notion that a man is only as good as his word, and a handshake can seal a deal, is alive and well throughout the reaches of the West.

White sands at Monahans: The "white sands," or simply "the sand" (in West Texas), extend about 40 miles from north-northeast to south-southwest across West Texas and the southeasternmost corner of New Mexico. At its widest, the sand is 20 miles, but in most places it is less than 10. The sand is the remnant of an ancient seacoast (after Permian time); it is particularly fine (and white) because it has experienced several cycles of weathering. The sand was a major barrier to east–west travel because wagons would get stuck in the dunes. When traveling westward toward the sand on an overcast day it seems the seacoast should be over the next horizon. The flora is of coastal grass variety; the color changes from the red sand of the High Plains to the sudden white of dunes; brackish lakes across the state line in New Mexico (a major salt-producing area) contribute the salty sea smell to complete the illusion that you are at the seacoast.

Monahans Sand Dunes State Park contains some of the most dramatic parts of the sand, with huge dunes resembling the Sahara and unusual flora and fauna. In spite of the seeming aridity of the area, in the basins at the bottoms of dunes there is water just below the surface; in some cases this water sustains small thickets of brush-trees. Indians dug water holes at such locations. The sand was a favorite hideout for Comanche raiders as entire herds could be fed on the grass and watered at the dug holes in places white men believed nothing could survive. The ill-fated "Nolan's Lost Expedition" which went for 86 hours without water reached their limit in the sand and turned back. Meanwhile, the Comanches they were pursuing watered themselves and their horses nearby.

Ranchers began to settle in the sand in the late 1880s — emboldened by the perfection of the windmill. Windmill sales and repairs were an early economic staple of Midland, the market center nearest the major ranches in the sand. Monahans, which grew up around a water well drilled in 1880 and utilized by the Texas Pacific the next year, was an oasis in the sand for early travelers. Successful drilling for petroleum began in the sand in the mid-1920s and today the sand is a major part of the Permian Basin petroleum producing region.

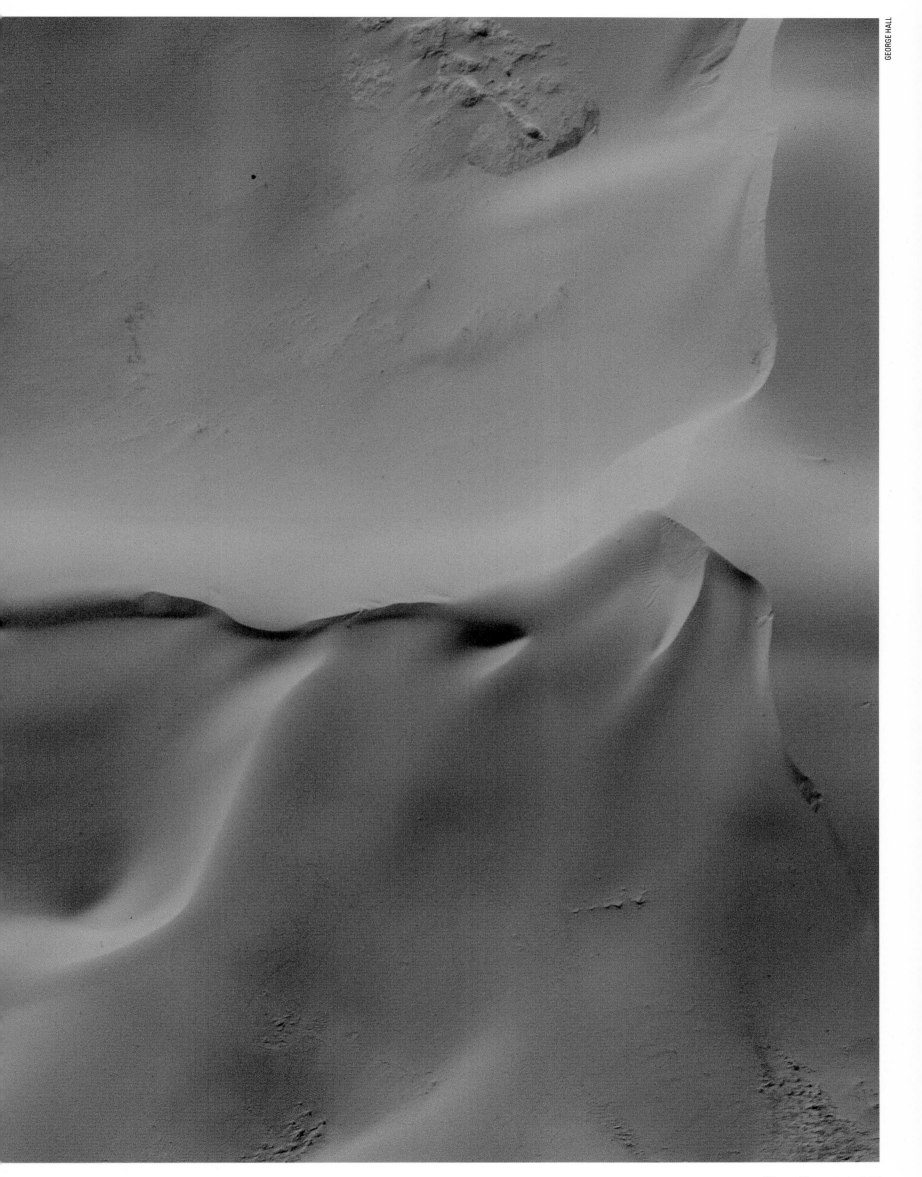

Odessa–Midland: The two cities are 20 miles apart in the geographic center of the 80,000 square mile petroleum producing region known as the Permian Basin of West Texas and Southeast New Mexico. One of the great petroleum producing regions on Earth, the Permian Basin is responsible for 20–25 percent of the total domestic oil and gas production; natural gas production from the Permian Basin reaches more than two-thirds of the U.S. population.

Midland had the highest per capita income in the United States in 1981 at $16,467; one-quarter of Midland's population holds a college degree. The work force is strongly managerial and focused in the many tall office buildings constructed downtown; Midland is the headquarters and the financial, and operations center of the Permian Basin. Its population increased to more than 90,000 during the most recent oil boom (the late 70s and early 80s). Now it is about 85,000. Major employers include large oil companies and independent operators, banks and legal firms. Many residents are independent oil operators, geologists, engineers and draftsmen. There is old land–cattle wealth in the form of a group of powerful families that arrived in the 1880s and hung on until oil was discovered. Midlanders tend to be circumspect with their wealth; homes that are unremarkable from the outside become dazzlers once you have gained admittance. During the last boom, Midland had the third-largest Rolls Royce dealership in the United States. Although Midlanders control, manage, and administrate the vast petroleum reserves, there are only small reserves in the county itself. Not so 20 miles west, toward its sister city and lifelong rival, Odessa.

Odessa is the blue-collar town of the Permian Basin. Named after the Russian wheat capital on the Volga, Odessa has few tall buildings and is more sprawling than Midland. It is also larger, with a population ranging from 110,000–125,000 according to the fortunes of the oil fields. It, too, is a rich town with a per capita income of $12,268 in 1981. It thus ranks behind Midland and Houston and ahead of Dallas. Odessa is the transportation, drilling, construction, well servicing, welding, and roughnecking headquarters of the Permian Basin. Its major employers tend to be oily-hands types; plastic and hydrocarbon plants are located south of the city. Odessa Permian High School has been a powerhouse of Texas schoolboy football for twenty years. Ector County is one of the top two oil-producing counties in Texas and the city of Odessa is checkerboarded with vacant lots which await the driller. Other lots already contain a pumpjack methodically moving up and down behind chain-link fences while children play in the remaining free space.

Lubbock: Lubbock, a modern city of 210,000, is the largest on the High Plains and one of the most important agribusiness centers in the world.

Left New subdivision outside Lubbock: Texans still prefer free-standing houses, though modern living is a far cry from the lonely ranch or farm houses of the pioneers. Modern housing patterns follow every style, a melange of cultural traditions. Plans for subdivisions today may be drawn up in San Francisco or New York, then copied coast to coast.

Sometime in the 1870s buffalo hunters began to camp in Yellow House Draw, on the site of modern Lubbock. There was a battle between hide-hunters and Indians in the draw as late as 1877. In 1879 a venturesome storekeeper, George W. Singer, established a trading post a few miles northwest of the present city, at the crossing of the Fort Griffin–Fort Sumner–Fort Elliot–Fort Stockton roads. In those days there were no towns and few ranches, and Army posts were the only points of reference on the High Plains. Singer prospered, and his family became the first white settlers in the area. Between about 1885–1895 the southern part of present Lubbock County was owned and developed by the IOA Ranch. As everywhere in West Texas and on the High Plains, big ranches dominated. These in Texas were more like modern corporations than the personal empires of stubborn pioneer cowmen (such as celebrated in many a Western movie). Above all, they were businesses. However many cowmen detested the closing of the frontier and the old frontier way of life—and above all hated the imposition of closed pastures with barbed wire, most ranch owners were businessmen first, defenders of rugged individualism second. With the ending of the old trail drives north to market, which were largely finished by the 1880s, most cattlemen welcomed the coming of railroads and settlers. This connected them with markets, and they usually had excess land to sell. They often possessed the capital to start a bank once there were enough customers in the territory. Cowboys on the High Plains, however, feared that the coming of farmers would bring sharecropping or tenantry to the West, and that with the hoe-men would come blacks — recreating the world of East Texas or the South, which many of them had fled to the "free" life in the West. Some of the first farmers who tried to plant cotton on the High Plains were roped and dragged by cowboys, who hoped to frighten them away.

But wire, rails, and cotton were inevitable, and the far-seeing made the best of it. Thus Rollie Burns, the last manager of the great IOA Ranch, was a founder of the City of Lubbock in 1891. The town, like the county, was named for Texas' great war-time (War Between the States, that is) governor, Francis Lubbock. The farmers began to arrive about 1905. Cotton quickly became a major crop. By 1909 a cotton gin had been established, and cotton was now the backbone of the local economy. What was created was nothing like the cotton plantations of East Texas or the Old South. Big farms grew up — in a general pattern getting bigger over the years as families died off or sold out — but in the modern pattern of agribusiness. High Plains farming required large acreages and capital investment as well as luck, hard work, and expertise. The strong held on through bad years and gradually grew stronger. Farms were and are still mostly family operations, though they may be organized as corporations for tax and legal purposes. And tenantry became common — but the modern tenant farmer usually owns land of his own with a great investment in equipment and may be a millionaire in his own right.

Lubbock is the cotton capital of Texas, the hub of an enormous agribusiness in grain sorghums and wheat as well. A military installation, Reese Air Force Base, is important, as are manufacturing, trucking, distributing, medicine, education, and petroleum — few places in the region are far from oil wells. Lubbock has also become the cultural center for the plains, with its universities and colleges and museums.

But the city has not strayed from the heritage on which it was built. The Ranching Heritage Center celebrates the history of the High Plains, as does the work of local musicians, among whom are Buddy Holly (Lubbock was his home town), Mac Davis, and John Denver.

Overleaf

Texas Tech University, Lubbock: The fastest growing, and thriving communities in Texas all have colleges or universities nearby. Texas Tech, a state university, was long called a "cow college" after its founding in 1925. Now one of the most important educational institutions in West Texas, Tech, with its Health Science Center since 1969, employs more than 1,800 faculty members and has an enrollment of more than 23,000 students. Lubbock Christian and South Plains Colleges are also in the city.

Left

Plains Coop, Lubbock: Texas has approximately 750 cotton gins; 33 of these are located in Lubbock County. The Plains Cooperative is the largest. Things have come a long way since Eli Whitney and the old local local gins that used to process perhaps 900 bales in a single season. Ginning is now a high-speed operation, handling a $1 billion crop of 4 million bales in a normal year.

Idalou Cotton Gin, near Lubbock: The ginning season continues long after picking time in the fall, with white-lint smoke pouring out day and night. The smoke may smell bad, like oil, but it means money in the bank.

Overleaf

Denver City: Denver City is not Denver, Colorado — but it does well enough. In Yoakum County southwest of Lubbock near the New Mexico border, it was founded because of oil. The Wasson Pool was discovered here in 1939, and the population swelled to more than 5,000 during the first boom years. After a decline in the bad-market era of the 1950s, the number has risen again to 4,704.
Yoakum County has produced more than 1 million barrels of oil; its proven reserves are worth more than $1 billion still, making Denver City the center of one of Texas' leading petroleum-producing counties.

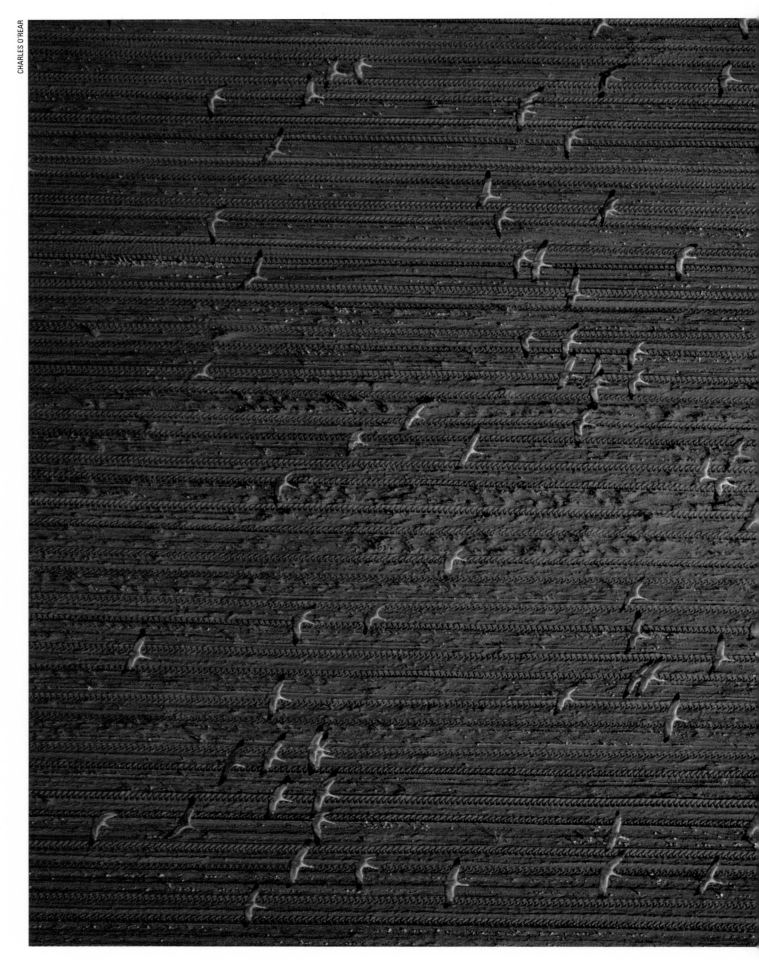

Sandhill cranes: One of the 540 species found in Texas, these great birds inhabit the sandy hills along the Pecos River of the Llano Estacado. They are not an endangered species, unlike the whooping cranes for which they have been used as surrogate mothers.

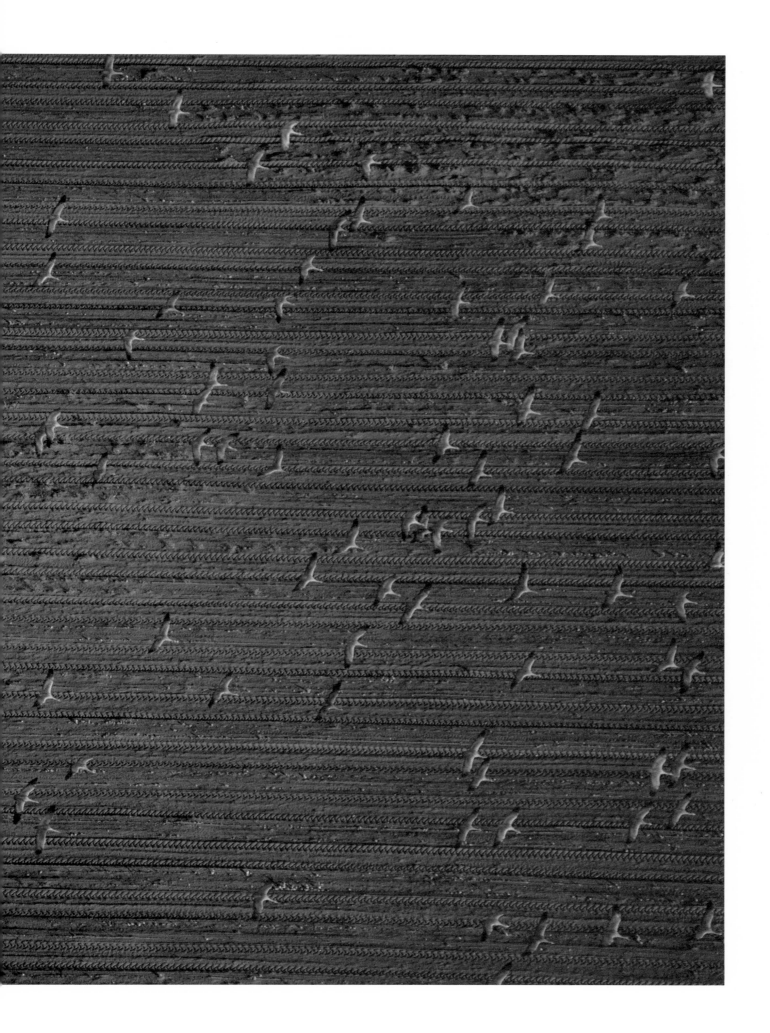

CHARLES O'REAR

Lamesa: An agribusiness and oil production center of some 12,000, Lamesa is typical of West Texas towns that appear along the major highways about every 30 miles, their low-rise buildings blending with the plains. The first settlement in the vicinity was the headquarters, with a post office, of the OTO Ranch. This was known as Chicago, in humorous deference to the fact that one of the owners hailed from that city. About two miles from Chicago another small community took root. Its name was derived from the Spanish, *la mesa,* meaning flat or tableland; however, article and noun were combined and the name is always pronounced in the English, not the Spanish, fashion. The two settlements merged by 1905, with Lamesa prevailing and becoming the seat of Dawson County.

Drilling near Lamesa.
The reddish earth around Lamesa is carved
into grain and cotton fields, most of which
sport oil wells.

Right

Cottonseed piled outside gin: Cottonseed is a by-product of cotton-ginning, which separates it from the fiber. But it is not a waste product; cottonseed ranks as an important cash crop in Texas. Production has ranged from 1.1 million to 2.4 million tons in recent years, with a value of $91.6 to $207.2 million. As with all commodities, the price fluctuates; when demand is high sale of cottonseed pays for the ginning process.

The end product is cottonseed oil. There are currently 20-odd cottonseed oil mills in the state, one of which is in Dawson County, near this site.

Above

Old church on Highway 84 near Justiceburg: West Texas was settled primarily by evangelical Protestants who came originally from the British Isles; the old-time religion was and is a very important part of the culture they brought with them. Before 1900 church groups rarely erected churches anywhere; communities gathered for camp meetings in brush arbors. Later, the various denominations built churches in the towns.

Justiceburg is in Garza County on the Double Mountains Fork of the Brazos River.

Right Train near Post: Railroads made West Texas as much as water and wire; cattlemen needed rails to avoid long cattle drives, and farming was impossible without this access to distant markets. Railroad men also encouraged (in fact, oversold) settlement in the west because they needed farmers and communities as customers; railroaders founded many towns. Despite the rise of trucking, which now hauls more goods, rails are still indispensable in this country. Enormously long trains, some pulled by three or more engines, are a common sight on the plains.

The nearby town of Post has an interesting history. It was founded by C. W. Post, the cereal king of "Post Toasties" fame. The obje was to create a model farming community of good rural people. In Post's town no liquor could be sold, no lots purchased by speculators, and high sanitation standards were enforced — all revolutionary ideas in the West of 1907. Post spent a fortune on the town, building most of the public facilities, including the Algerita Hotel and a textile mill that still operates. Between 1910-1913 he invested more than $50,000 in various rain-making experiments, all of which failed. In poor health, Post killed himself in 1914.

Stored drilling pipe, Snyder: Oil drilling requires thousands of miles of pipe, and the making, selling, and delivery of steel pipe is a major enterprise across Texas.

Snyder (population 12,705) is the seat of Scurry County, one of the state's leading petroleum producers — the county for some years has supplied 3 percent of the U.S. total. The town grew up around William Henry "Pete" Snyder's store, established in 1876; it was called "Robber's Roost," whether because of the nature of Pete's merchandizing practices or the character of early denizens is not clear.

Snyder laid out a real town in 1882, which became the county seat in 1884. Oil was found in 1923, and major production began after 1948 with the discovery of the Canyon Reef Formation, one of the bonanzas of the Permian Basin.

Oil well northwest of Snyder, Scurry County: The uninitiated are impressed by oil derricks in Texas; those who know the oil business much prefer the sight of pumpjacks. A rising and falling pumpjack — pumping up thick, black crude — is the symbol of success. The derrick is the wildcatter's symbol. And a drilling rig means enormous investment with a statistically small chance of success: at least eight holes blow dust or hit salt water for every one that brings up oil.

Many banks across the Permian Basin of West Texas use oil field logos or symbology on their letterheads. Most of them (and some now and again to their sorrow) are heavily involved in the petroleum business, and the preferred logo is always a pumpjack, never a derrick or drilling rig.

Salt Fork of the Brazos River south of Jayton, Kent County: Like many of the mineral-choked streams of West Texas, the Salt Fork has a bitter taste, which was first discovered by Albert Pike, who passed this way in 1832 on an expedition out of New Mexico. Albert Pike is not to be confused with Zebulon, who named Pike's Peak in Colorado and also came through Texas years earlier.

Not many passed this way until 1909 when the town of Jayton was established by J. B. Jay, cattleman, and R. A. Jay, banker and real estate promoter. In 1952 the town won a bitter election to take the county seat away from Clairemont, although it required some years of litigation to achieve the move. The size of the vote may be judged by the fact that the population of Jayton is now 638.

Fields, Haskell County.

Haskell County lies on the North Central or Rolling Plains, an agricultural region with some oil activity. There are about 7,000 residents, half of whom live in Haskell, the county seat. This area was a favorite camping place for the Comanches and Kiowas. The Marcy expedition explored it in 1849, stopping at Willow Springs. A member of the party wrote such a glowing description of the country that in 1879 — the Indians gone — Thomas Tucker sought it out, building the first house at a spot he called Rice

Springs. When the county was organized in 1885, Tucker became the first county judge. However, he escaped immortality when the post office renamed the station Haskell, after a Texas hero martyred at Goliad in 1836.
The first store in the town of Haskell sold groceries and whiskey. The "Road to Ruin" saloon doubled as the town church on Sunday mornings. Haskell is now a quiet farm trading center, dealing in cotton, grains, beef cattle and hogs.

Right
Vernon: Vernon is a neatly laid-out agribusiness and oil centre between the Pease River and Paradise Creek, both tributaries of the Prairie Dog Fork of the Red River that serves as the Texas-Oklahoma boundary. The town holds 12,695 of Wilbarger County's 16,000 people. Besides cotton, wheat and alfalfa, which bring in some $35 million from 24,000 irrigated acres hereabouts, and oil, which produces $63 million in income, Vernon manufactures boots, clothing and guar products. It also has a junior college.

County courthouse, Haskell.

Cattle pen, Waggoner Ranch

The Waggoner Ranch, located on the Rolling Plains near the Oklahoma border is one of the finest operations in Texas. And behind it lies a true tale of empire making.

Daniel Waggoner, the founder, was about 22 when he began running cattle on Denton Creek. In 1850 he acquired 15,000 acres at Cactus Hill on the Trinity River in Wise County, stocking them with 242 longhorns and six horses. This was typical of 1850s Texas, when land was limitless along the settlement frontier, men were beginning to think about cattle, and good horses were still scarce.

However, Cactus Hill was exposed to Comanche raiding, and Daniel was forced to pull back to Denton Creek. The Indian threat grew worse during the Civil War, and immediately following the conflict northwest Texas was filled with poor, restless, and desperate men, some deserters from both armies. To the Indian problem was added wholesale stock stealing.

About 1866 Waggoner began to use the Three D brand — three "Ds" in reverse — which was easy to recognize but difficult to burn or change. By this time longhorn range cattle were common in Texas, but there was no local market in the ruined South. Cattle could be sold profitably in Missouri; however, driving them to that state was extremely dangerous because both numerous gangs of border desperadoes and the Missourans preyed on Texas drovers; herds that were not stampeded by bandits met with quarantines and legal obstacles. However, as railroads moved westward across Kansas, Texas cattlemen found they could drive herds directly to railheads from which cattle could be shipped to the insatiable stockyards of Chicago.

No drive was easy: The distances were huge, the terrain covered with both human and natural obstacles such as rivers and long stretches without decent water. But the rewards could be immense. Steers that were almost worthless on the Texas plains sold from $16 to $20 a head in Kansas. Ranchers that took the risk and carried through could make as much as $20,000 in a single season, an immense sum on the frontier. The trail drives became an imperishable part of Western history and legend, and Daniel Waggoner was part of it.

He and his partner son, William Thomas, gathered a herd in Clay County on the Red River just across from the Indian Territory in 1869; they wintered the herd there and got the jump on all the other trail herds in the spring of 1870. The Waggoners hit the early market, and the profit they made was the basis of one of the greatest ranching fortunes in Texas.

As the Comanches and Kiowas were driven back to their final fastnesses on the High Plains, the Waggoners pushed westward. The ranch headquarters was moved northwest to a site on the Wichita River in Wichita County. From here the ranch spread out, even leasing lands north of the Red River. Daniel and his son understood that the day of open range and trail drives would soon end, and they began buying title to the land they required.

They also saw that the era of the longhorn and range stock was over, and the Three D was among the very first to start breeding shorthorn and English Hereford cattle. At the same time the ranch became famous for the quality of its horseflesh. By 1903, the ranch ran 60,000 head of improved stock on 1 million acres and was served by three different railroads.

Daniel Waggoner, who had seen the start and close of an era, died in 1904. The W. T. Waggoner Ranch, as it was now called after William Thomas, began to sell off portions to farmers. It was split into four great but manageable divisions: White Face, Four Corners, Santa Rosa, and Zacaweista. In 1909 W. T. divided the ranch among his three children, Paul, Guy, and daughter Electra.

On April Fools Day, 1911, a water-drilling crew struck oil near the small town named for Electra Waggoner, bringing in the Electra Field and setting off one of the wildest oil booms in Texas history. This also made the Waggoners immensely richer; they developed their own refinery and a chain of service stations, the Three D.

In 1923 all the properties were merged into the Waggoner Estate — again a move anticipating trends — and the management is in the hands of a trustee and board of directors.

Waggoner Ranch, Wichita County

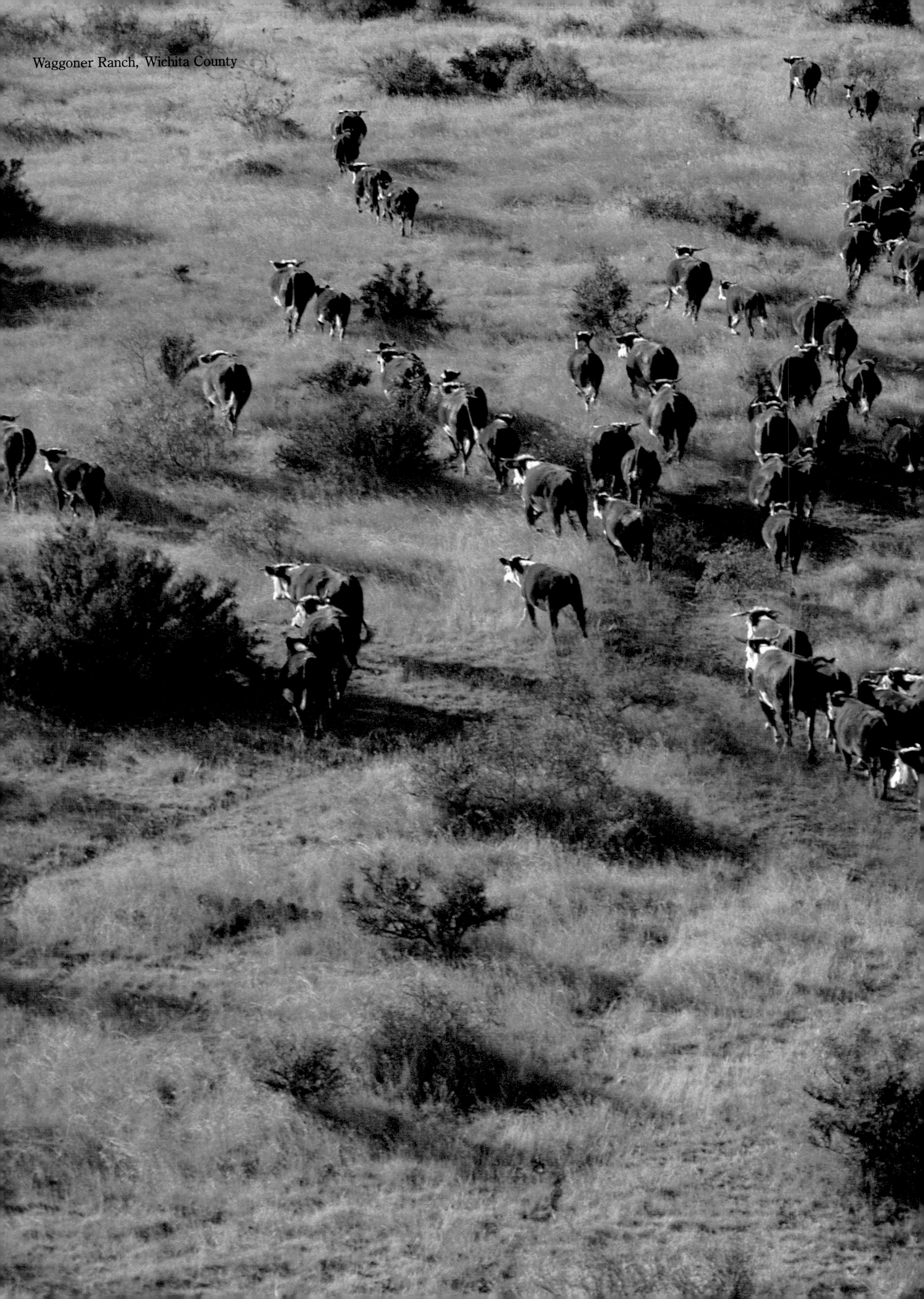

Wichita Falls: Luck, the main chance, and a scent of empire have always hung over Wichita Falls, Texas, now a metropolitan area of 130,000, a major oil center sprawling across three county lines.

It may be legend, but in 1837 the area of the original town site was won in a poker game by J. A. Scott of Missouri. But it was then a cheap bet; the owner might have legal title, however the land itself was still in the possession of the Indians. Scott probably forgot all about the deed, but after his death in 1854 his heirs were determined to look into it. After the Comanches were driven from the plains in 1876, Scott's heirs dispatched M. W. Seeley to map a town site and prepare the land for development.

When Seeley arrived at the five-foot falls on the Wichita — named for a Plains tribe that was powerful in the eighteenth century but vanished soon afterward — he found two white men living in the vicinity. One was Tom Buntin, a buffalo hunter; the other was called John Weeler. Seeley drew up his town site, although dreams were running far ahead of reality. While the town was plotted in 1876, showing not only the falls of the river but grandiose projections of wharves to be built to service steamboats, the first permanent settlers, J. H Barwise and family, did not arrive until December, 1879. Others soon came to the prairie, however, and Wichita County was organized in 1882. In the same year, townspeople donated half of their property along the right of way to persuade the Fort Worth and Denver Railroad to alter its course

ive miles, bringing rails to the settlement. This semi-blackmail was often practised in the West and usually eagerly subscribed to by the people. The first train out, however, carried only buffalo bones for fertilizer.

The first brick and masonry buildings were erected in 1883; the best-known (and requented) was the White Elephant saloon. The town then remained a ranching and arming center until 1911, when Electra Waggoner's oil field made it the hub of an oil boom.

Oil built Wichita Falls and remained the base of its economy. The wild oil-rush years, however, gave it a reputation as a place for get-rich-quick schemes, high rollers, and outright swindlers. In one deal, investors were sold shares in a major, four-storey office building. The promoters fulfilled the contract by erecting a four-storey edifice measuring 10 feet by 16 feet — hardly big enough, as it was said, for an outhouse. This building, put up in 1919, still stands vacant as the "world's littlest skyscraper."

The junior college established during the first oil boom became four-year Hardin College in 1946, Midwestern University in 1950. It entered the state university system in 1961 and has an enrollment of about 5,000.

Oil is still dominant, but Sheppard Air Force Base, manufacturing, distribution, and agribusiness are also significant additions to the economy.

Overleaf New suburb, Abilene: The explosion of oil drilling in the 1970s vastly expanded the oil-field services industry in Abilene, which is geographically situated to serve both the north-central Texas fields and the eastern edge of the Permian Basin. At the same time, diversified manufacturing — making clothing, trailers, building materials, aircraft parts, electronics, cans, and processing agribusiness products — outstripped the total income received from petroleum and petroleum services.

All this has led to rapid growth and expansion of housing in the Abilene metropolitan area.

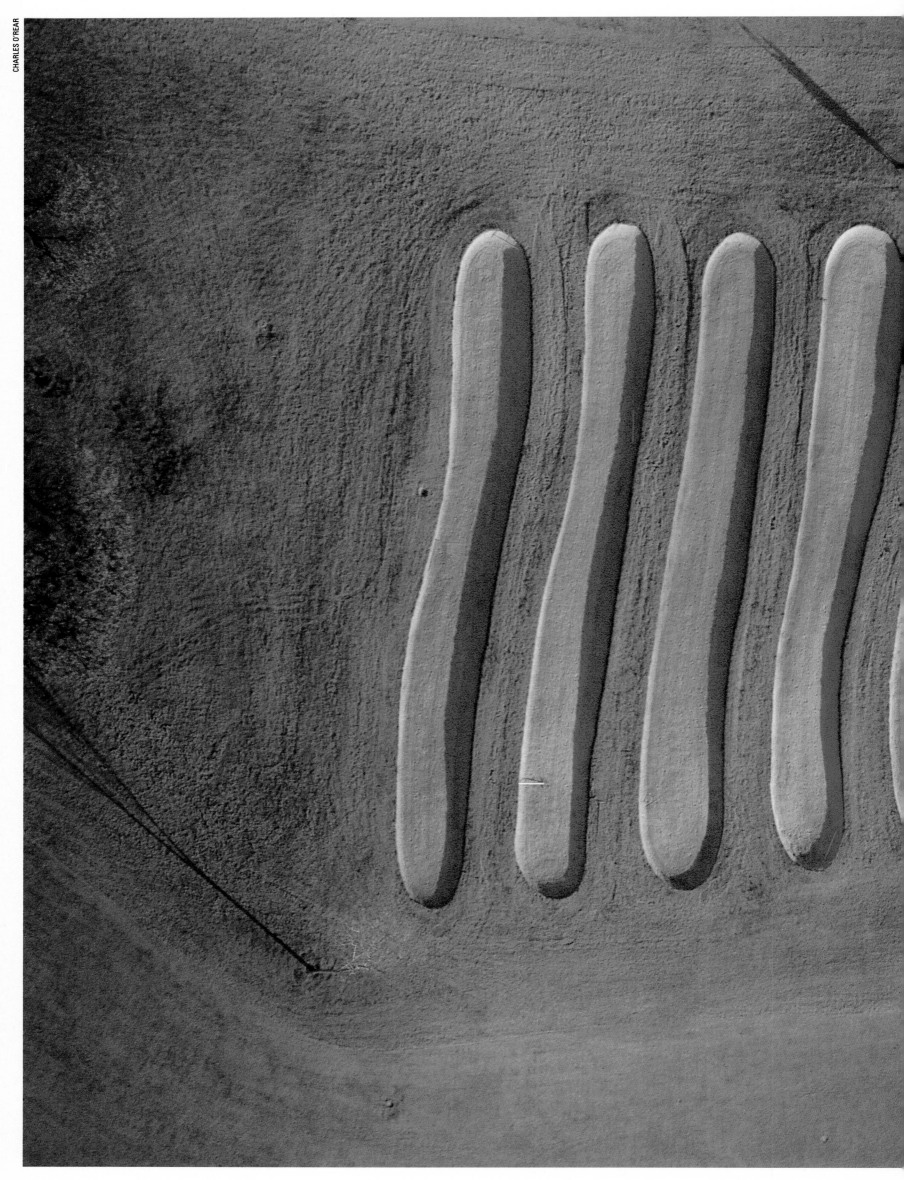

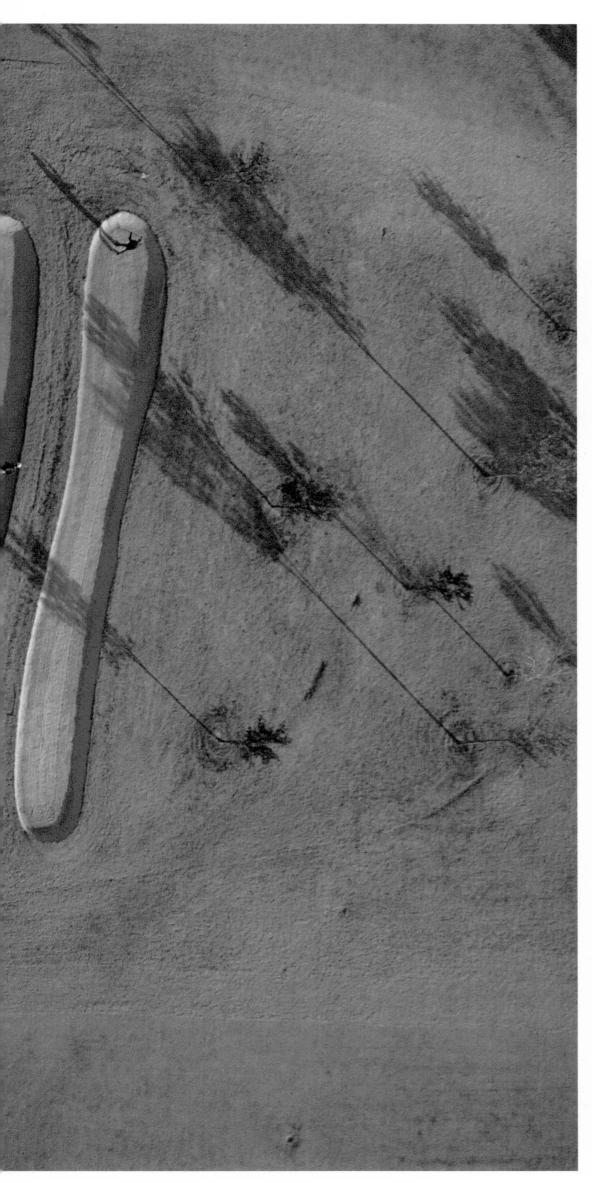

Sand traps, Fairway Oaks Golf Course, Abilene: Prosperity has brought all the appurtenances of modern civilization to West Texas, and this includes the devilish game invented by the Scots some centuries back. Fairways and greens require continual watering in this climate, and water hazards are almost always artificial — but there is no shortage of the materials to make sand traps for the duffer. In fact, sand and gravel are major products of Taylor County, of which Abilene is the seat.

Abilene: A modern metropolitan area of some 110,000, Abilene is a crossroads and a nexus for a vast region. Highways and railroads meet here, where several regions of Texas join. South of Abilene there is a line of hills known as the Callahan Divide, separating the Brazos River watershed from that of the Colorado and also separating the Rolling Plains of north-central Texas from the Edwards Plateau. And Abilene is on the east–west division of the state where rainfall runs out.

The city services oil activities to the north, all the way to the Oklahoma fields, as well as the intense activity in the eastern Permian Basin, to the north-northwest. Agribusiness is mostly dry-land farming and ranching, with about 80 percent of income derived from stock; this is almost as much as the income from oil.

There is a break in the Callahan Divide through which the vast bison herds used to pass on their migrations from the North Central Plains down to the Edwards Plateau. Ancient Paleo-Indian hunters gathered here, roasting their kills in great kitchen middens in the rock; later hunters named this Buffalo Gap. When cattlemen moved into the area after the Civil War, a settlement here became the county se when Taylor County was organized in 1878. But when the Texas and Pacific Railroad avoided Buffalo Gap and established a shippin point at present Abilene (named for the old end-o'-track in Kansas) in 1881, settlers and business gravitated there.

Overleaf

Mobile home park, northwest Abilene: Mobile home parks may have first taken solid root in California, but they are now a feature of the restless, expanding Sunbelt everywhere. Seen by some as substitute, temporary housing, they have become a permanent feature around most Texas cities where other types of home ownership are beyond the financial reach of most transients and many kinds of working people. Quite elaborate sites have also been developed for retirees.

In Abilene and most West Texas cities, the great proliferation of mobile homes came with the 1970s oil boom. Blight or boon, they are proving to be a permanent fixture on the outskirts of towns, where land can still be acquired and zoning regulations do not bar their presence.

CHARLES O'REAR

Interchange, Winters Freeway, Abilene:
Abilene faces north and south, east and west.
Highways as well as rails connect the city with
the oil fields and ranches. Abilene's major
economic ties have always been with sister
cities to the west: Midland–Odessa, Big
Spring, and San Angelo. They are all partners
in Abilene's oil-field service business. The city
is also joined with them through high-school
athletic districts (rivalry and sports feuds are
intense), family ties, television stations, and
transportation links.

Westgate Mall parking lot, Abilene: The shopping mall came late to Texas after its introduction to the East Coast — and the true, all-family, all-day emporium and American cultural center may yet be in its infancy here. But nowhere has its growth become more noticeable or its impact more profound. The splendid highway system facilitates its growth, to the detriment of most downtown centers. Across much of Texas the new air-conditioned mall has replaced the general store, and the parking lot has replaced the hitching post.

WEST TEXAS ☆ 147

Abilene Christian University: Abilene is in West Texas and looks toward West Texas, but the city's very conservative religious–political–cultural roots stem from North and East Texas. The city's three institutions of higher learning have always been church-affiliated. If in other parts such connections have been loosened or decayed, here the ties still bind. Abilene Christian University, founded by the Church of Christ in 1906, has some 4,500 students, all of whom are expected to respect traditional values. McMurry College is Methodist, and Hardin-Simmons University is a Southern Baptist stronghold.

Such influences have always made Abilene appear more straight-laced (or narrow-minded, depending on the view) than most conservative West Texas towns. For many years Abilene had no liquor, sparking controversies up to the

present. Also, it had no Mexicans or blacks. The new common-wall townhouses sprouting in West Abilene, however, show the intrusion of outside cultural forces with the influx of both new people and new money. Culturally as well as economically and geographically, Abilene is in a transition from old to new. Probably a lot of the new will take root — but much of the old will always remain.

Drilling rig north of Trent, Taylor County:
Trent, Texas, lies northwest of Buzzard
Mountain and almost due west of Abilene in
the northwest corner of Taylor County. This
isolated rig in lonesome country symbolizes
Texas' production of 920 million barrels of oil
per year, first in the nation. Alaska is now a
close second. The leading producing counties
are Gregg (East Texas, Longview, 2.8 billion
barrels total), and Ector (Permian Basin,
Odessa, 2.4 billion). Oil has been produced
since the 1880s; the early stories mainly
revolve around the frustration of people drilling
holes for water and striking oil. And the early
finds, however fabulous, came in days when
the stuff sold for 3 cents a barrel.

Today oil does much better and the search for
it is a leading enterprise, although most of it
has been found. Texas production has steadily
declined since 1972, and proven reserves have
not increased since 1967.

Texas still has the largest proven liquid
hydrocarbon reserves — 10.7 billion barrels,
29.4 percent of the total — as well as natural
gas, often found with oil. And it has, by far, the
largest refining capacity in the nation.

CHARLES O'REAR

Feedlot near Trent, Taylor County: Along with oil and gas, Texas is the agribusiness giant of the nation — leading all other states in the number of farms and ranches, farm and ranchland acreage, cattle slaughtered, cattle on feed, calf births, sheep and lambs slaughtered, goats, cash receipts from livestock farming, cattle and calves, beef cows, sheep and lambs, wool and mohair production, exports of tallow and lard. But many Texans do not realize that the state now ranks above such historic leaders as Nebraska and Iowa in the number of cattle on feed at commercial feedlots.

Range beef that not too long ago was sent north to fatten for market is now finished nicely at dozens of isolated West Texas feedlots.

North Texas

North Texas is a term of convenience for the section of Texas in the far north-central portion of the state that lies between the Cross Timbers on the west and the Piney Woods on the east. It is clearly part of neither East nor West Texas. It is dominated by two large cities, Dallas and Fort Worth.

These rise from broad, almost treeless prairies and clayish blacklands, rich plains easily broken by the plow and which from before the Civil War until the 1930s were ruled by cotton. This was a heavily populated country of smaller farms, part of the old farming heartland of Texas. However, the prairies surrendered the cotton crown to the huge, irrigated and mechanized plantations of the High Plains long ago, turning to a more diversified farming and livestock raising, and above all, to service industries and manufacturing in the cities.

Dallas and Fort Worth anchor, east and west, a metropolitan urban area known as the Metroplex, in which many smaller but rapidly growing incorporated cities play key roles: Arlington (160,000) with its Texas Rangers baseball team and Six Flags; Garland (139,000) with its industrial parks; Irving (110,000) near the airport, home of Texas Stadium and Las Colinas; and Grand Prairie, Richardson, and Plano, all with populations of more than 70,000. These cities are all economically joined, though they spread across three counties; they are part of a whole.

Dallas — Big D — is the heart and hub, although each community has a distinct place and life of its own. Dallas is a modern success story. It began as a trading post on the Trinity River, emerged as a major cotton-farming center, became an agribusiness center with important agricultural publications and associations. But the community soon diversified, creating one of the most vibrant economies in the world. Without significant petroleum, the fuel of so much Texas growth and progress, Dallas raised itself almost by its bootstraps from the plain, through banking and insurance enterprises, transportation, electronics manufacturing, data processing, conventions, and trade fairs and shows. The second largest city in Texas, it ranks seventh in the United States with more than 900,000 in-city inhabitants.

Dallas has home offices of more insurance companies than any city, and it is headquarters for 657 firms with net assets of $1 million or more, ranking third in this respect in the nation. It is the national leader in conventions, which bring in a half billion dollars annually. The Metroplex itself has more than 1,100 such businesses: 80 companies listed on the New York Stock Exchange, and some 5,000 manufacturing plants that turn out every product from high fashion to high tech. More than 1.5 million visitors attend the conventions and trade shows, making Dallas first in tourism in Texas.

The Dallas–Fort Worth International Airport makes the Metroplex a crossroads for the United States, a hub of the Sunbelt, and an important destination on the north–south international route.

All modern, complex economies are closely tied to education, and the Dallas area supports some 20 colleges and universities, including Southern Methodist University and branches of the University of Texas in both liberal arts and medicine.

Dallas is a financial and insurance center, a great commercial city, an industrial region, and a sports center — a national leader in every category.

But the Dallas skyline, however, glowing and increasing month by month, stands for something more than statistics and commerce.

Dallas has created an opening to the world, but it is still a quintessentially Texan city, founded and peopled largely by Texans. The old ethic and new life styles combine. The modern corporation, aerospace and computers, have met and merged with the cotton and cattle kingdoms of the old frontier, creating new frontiers whose impact will be felt far from North Texas all across the world.

Six Flags Over Texas, Arlington: Six flags have waved over Texas, though the tenure of some, especially the French, was tenuous. And that historical fact sets the theme of this giant amusement park at Arlington on Highway 360, just off Interstate 30. The 205 acres are divided into six sections, each reflecting in some way the six nations and peoples who have claimed Texas: the Spanish, French, Mexican, Republic of Texas, the Confederacy, and the United States of America.

More than 100 rides are offered, such as the impressive rollercoaster shown here, and shows, exhibits, and other attractions. A single charge gives admission to all the rides. Since its opening, Six Flags has become Texas' biggest tourist attraction — few leave Dallas without visiting it. More than 40 million people have passed through its gates.

Dallas–Fort Worth International Airport: The largest and most ambitious air terminal in the world, covering some 17,000 acres, DFW was subjected to much criticism when it opened in January 1974. Many thought the airport was too big, too spread out — connections between terminals are by rail — and above all, too far away from downtown Dallas and Fort Worth. That has changed as business has escalated, requiring the building of new space. In effect, cities have grown up around it. In addition to being a major air hub, Dallas is also headquarters for several major airlines. Although "Dallas" appears first in the name, the airport is in Tarrant, not Dallas County, and it is closer to Fort Worth as well as Irving and other major cities within the Metroplex. Once believed to be too far away, the complex is becoming a city in itself.

Southfork Ranch: The 'Southfork Ranch' made famous by the CBS television series 'Dallas' — which is about as representative of the city and its people as most things on TV — was the privately owned Duncan Ranch in Collin County, located on Farm Road 2551 northeast of Dallas.

Leased by the production as an exterior location for filming, the ranch is open to the public, for an admission charge, weekdays from noon to five. Due to the popularity of the series, visitors come from all over the United States and overseas. Thousands want to see 'Southfork', the home of the Ewings, and 'J.R.'s office building', which is really 2001 Bryan Tower in downtown Dallas. Tours are not permitted inside the main house, however.

In 1984 the property was purchased by a realty company, and will eventually be used for commercial development.

New homes, Las Colinas, Irving.

GEORGE HALL

New construction, Dallas.

GEORGE HALL

Las Colinas (Spanish, "The Hills") is a Texas-sized pioneer development that has been cited as a model for the future, and in fact has been imitated elsewhere. Las Colinas is being developed on 12,000 acres within the city of Irving; the area is a former ranch that became city-locked by the explosive growth of the Metroplex. The community, a series of "villages," provides residences, workplaces, and recreational facilities for businesses and their owners and executives. This is strictly middle and upper-middle income housing: When the project began, homes were available for $80,000 but now run from well into six figures to more than $1 million.

Special efforts have been made to fit roads, paving, and drainage into the natural contours of the land, preserving as much beauty as possible. Construction is regulated; security is tight, with each home monitored by computer. There is a proposed overhead monorail system, and many homes are to be connected by canals — a feature inspired by San Antonio's River Walk.

By mid-1982 Las Colinas had 11,000 residents, 200 corporate offices, and a work force of 25,000.

Left:

Dallas skyline at night: The glowing glass towers reflect the growing importance of the city as a financial, industrial, and fashion center, whose wealth, power, and influence is increasingly recognized across the whole world.

Left Private aircraft, Love Field, Dallas: Vast distances, wealth, and excellent flying weather most of the year have all created a Texan love affair with the airplane. Military aviation was born in Texas at Fort Sam Houston in 1911, and some of the best-known air bases such as Randolph, Kelly, and Lackland have trained thousands of pilots over the years. Love Field was first established by the Army in 1914 (making it one of the oldest) and was named for Lt. M. L. Love, killed in a training flight in 1913. It became a civilian airport between the wars and reverted again to that status in 1950.

When Fort Worth expanded Midway Airport after World War II, local pride in Dallas demanded a massive development of Love Field. Between 1959–1965 this was Texas' premier airport with almost half of all boardings in the state. However, pressure upon facilities and safety considerations led to the construction of the Dallas–Fort Worth International Airport in 1974.
But Love Field did not die. It became the nexus of commuter airlines such as Southwest, and it is the preferred terminal for Texans flying in and out of Dallas.

BILL ELLZEY

Above Palatial Texas home, Dallas: There is no such thing as a "Dallas house," but fine homes abound. Every style of architecture, new and old, is used, but with a Sunbelt flavor: homes are fully air-conditioned, and they have lawn sprinkler systems and the inevitable pool. The large house is alive and well in Texas, despite the incursion of condominiums and townhomes. And the continuing construction of great houses creates a market for fine furnishings, modern and antique, and has even revived interest in that one-time adjunct of home culture, the grand piano.

Fort Worth: Fort Worth ("Where the West Begins") like so many Texas frontier settlements, was originally an army post; unlike most, it grew into a great city. And while only some 30 miles west of Dallas, Fort Worth was utterly different from Dallas in the early days. Dallas looked east and was built on cotton; Fort Worth was the gateway to Jacksboro and Palo Pinto, where the Texas West really began, and it thrived on cattle. The seat of Tarrant County, named for an Indian-fighting general, organized in 1850 when ranchers began to move onto the plains, Fort

Worth was an outfitting point for buffalo hunters and cattle drives. Then it became the cattle-marketing center for the state. But today its Western outlook (like Dallas' vaunted cosmopolitanism) is something of a put-on, for the old "cowtown" is a thoroughly modern American city in all respects.

Fort Worth is the western anchor of the Dallas–Fort Worth Metroplex — a mercantile, commercial, banking, finance, insurance, manufacturing, and wholesale trade centre for most of West Texas. The city is big in aerospace, airplane and helicopter

manufacturing. With almost 400,000 people, it is the fourth-largest city in Texas. Besides that, Fort Worth is an important education center, with Texas Christian University and other colleges, and an outstanding cultural center in its own right.

And where many older cities are now much decayed at the core, corporate enterprise and local pride have combined to restore much of the downtown, creating a model for other cities.

Fort Worth stockyards: After the Civil War, Fort Worth became the cattle capital of Texas. At first it was only a point on the Chisholm Trail, but residents put up the money to extend the Texas and Pacific Railroad tracks from Dallas after the line went bankrupt. In 1878 the Livestock Exchange began operations. The Western Cattle Trail made its terminus at Fort Worth, and the town could claim the titles of "Cowtown" and "Where the West Begins." By 1902, its hold on the cattle shipping and processing industry was solidified, when Armour and Swift built major packing plants adjoining the stockyards.

After World War II transportation changes led to the building of packing plants nearer to feedlots, and the stockyards declined. Today they are really more of a historical preservation than a business. The old Stock Exchange is now an art gallery, and the coliseum next door, the site of the first indoor rodeo (1917) and opera tenor Caruso's Texas debut, is now used only for small affairs. The Fat Stock Show and major rodeos have gone to the Will Rogers Coliseum elsewhere. Cattle are still bought and sold, but the packing plants have been demolished or turned into restaurants; most of the stockyard area is devoted to the tourist trade, with shops, bootmakers, and sellers of Western wear. Continual restoration goes on: 100,000 squar feet of an old barn and cattle-holding lot have been made into Billy Bob's Texas, billed as th world's largest nightclub.

Many people in Western clothes still throng t stockyards, but sadly, the real cowboys, like the cows, left long ago.

BILL ELZEY

Texas Stadium, Irving, home of the Dallas Cowboys: One of the winningest teams in the professional National Football League, the Dallas Cowboys were organized by the Murchison family in 1960. Although the Cowboys did not win a game their first year and had five losing seasons, they were able to force Lamar Hunt's Dallas Texans to move and become the Kansas City Chiefs. Since then, they have gone to the Super-Bowl five times (winning in 1972 and 1978) and advanced to the play-offs in 17 of 18 seasons. Sometimes billed as "America's Team," the Cowboys regularly lead in attendance and Neilsen ratings when games are televised. The team accounts for more than half of the sales of all NFL-licensed souvenirs. The Murchisons recently sold the franchise to a local group for $60 million.

Texas Stadium was planned and built by the organization while early seasons were played at the Cotton Bowl in Dallas, using a then controversial financial scheme: Stadium bonds had to be purchased by anyone wanting a season ticket to the games. But with the team's success, the rights to season seats are now a valuable commodity. The costly enclosed private boxes that form the second tier of the stadium are among the most prestigious properties in Texas.

BILL ELLZEY

Texas football: Sports of all sorts are big in Texas. The state, like a sovereign nation, maintains its own Sports Hall of Fame, honoring athletes such as Ben Hogan (golf), Rogers Hornsby and Tris Speaker (baseball), and Mildred (Babe) Didrikson (all-round woman athlete). The Southwest Athletic Conference, primarily Texas college teams, has recently dominated NCAA sports, winning three national championships, three second-place, and four third-place finishes in 1983. But the sport closest to Texan hearts is clearly football.

Football is not just a professional or collegiate activity. It is almost a religion in many communities. Football programs start in grade school, and some seventh-graders, fully equipped, vie before paying spectators. High-school games evoke keen rivalry between towns and districts and even widely separated areas of the state; the system is highly organized and regional play-offs determine annual champions in various categories according to school size.

While all this has been criticized as detracting from education, public interest and support produces a vast number of good players across Texas and makes the Southwest Football Conference a continuing national powerhouse. On crisp fall weekends, the gridirons come alive with bands, color, and derring-do from the Red River to the Rio Grande.

Central Texas

Austin: The state capital is in almost the geographic center of Texas. That was one reason Austin, named for the father of Texas, was made the capital of the Republic of Texas in 1839; the other reason is that the expansionist-minded President Lamar wanted to pull settlement to what was then the frontier. But for a time the population of Austin, including bureaucrats and wandering Comanches, was less than 1,000.

Until the 1970s this pleasant small city on the Colorado River was supported by government and education and enlivened only by the antics of legislators and the roar of fall football games. The not-for-profit payroll is still huge, politicians still act the same, and the University of Texas at Austin is a perennial football power. But the city has begun to change greatly. The presence of the university, high-technology research, the Sunbelt syndrome, the Texas business and tax climate and the attractiveness of the town itself have made Austin one of the hottest growth properties in the nation. Now 350,000, with new buildings going up all over, Austin has expanded over the blacklands prairie below the Balcones Scarp and through the limestone hills to become a genuine metropolitan area.

Above and right The University of Texas at Austin: Texas has 155 colleges and universities, enrolling some 750,000 students. Probably the best known, however, is the University of Texas at Austin, which is actually the flagship of a vast system that operates universities and health-science centers across the state. UT–Austin began classes in 1883 on 40 acres near the state Capitol. Sometimes embroiled in politics over the years, the university, now engulfed by the city of Austin, has not only survived but is steadily moving toward world-class status. The campus, once celebrated as a marriage mart for students, now attracts Nobel laureates, famous literary collections, 48,000 students, and high-technology research.

The future of the university was assured in 1923, when the Santa Rita No. 1 oil well was drilled on its vast landholdings in West Texas. The development of the Permian Basin stemming from that find has provided UT–Austin with one of the largest endowments in the country, and more recently, the university has developed significant private support.

Landmarks known to most Texans on the campus are the bell tower, made notorious by a crazed sniper in 1966, the football field, and the Lyndon B. Johnson Presidential Library.

State Capitol, Austin: When the old capitol burned down in 1881, Texans were determined to replace it with the biggest and best capitol in the land. They did, although it took the help of imported Scottish stone masons, convict labor, and the laying of special railroads. The legislature had to trade ten counties in the Panhandle to some Chicagoans to cover the cost of construction. Made of pink granite mined in Central Texas, the new Capitol opened for business in 1888. The dome stands seven feet higher than the National Capitol in Washington, D.C.: Texans planned it that way.

The building houses the state Legislature and key officers and is visited by many sightseers and tourists, only a few of whom are lobbyists.

Texas A & M University, College Station: Texas A & M is in what some consider the boondocks of Central Texas, and Aggie jokes are a Texas institution. But the modern A & M is no joke; it is a great university growing greater. Like rival UT–Austin, it's the centerpiece of a large state university system.

The university was authorized in 1871 and opened in 1876, the first state-supported land grant college in Texas. Historically, Texas A & M produced agrarians, civil engineers, and more Army officers than West Point. While it still does all those things, the university has changed greatly over the years: It is coeducational, increasingly devoted to the liberal arts, attracts many city girls and boys, and has a respected academic press.

The Corps of Cadets and football traditions are still important, however, and Aggies form a loyal band of alumni for life.

GEORGE HALL

Quarry near Austin: Petroleum products bring in the most money, but Texas is also a leading producer and consumer of non-fuel minerals such as stone, sand and gravel, and cement, with a total value of more than $1.5 billion in 1982.

Central Texas and the Edwards Plateau are particularly rich in limestone, granite, and dolomite rock, which are used in the making of crushed stone. Vast amounts of these minerals are extracted and used in the manufacture of cement, as aggregate for concrete, and not least, as road material for Texas' enormous network of highways. Lime is also an important product derived from stone. Sand and gravel is usually found along stream beds or terraces; Texas pits shipped 44 million short tons in 1982.

BILL ELZEY

arlos lignite mine, near College Station: Texas not usually thought of as a coal-producing ate. However, in the days before natural gas d oil were developed as energy sources, nite and bituminous coal were widely mined east and central Texas; many abandoned allow mine shafts still exist. And today xas, with enormous reserves of strippable nite, a low-rank coal, is becoming one of the rgest coal-producing regions. In 1980 30.2 million tons were extracted and rapidly increasing activity is expected to raise this to 46.4 million tons in 1985.

The lignite seams being worked are within 200 feet of the surface, where mouth-mine operations are economically feasible. Most of the lignite now mined is burned for electrical power generation by utilities, but new industrial uses are constantly being developed.

Canyon Lake, Comal County: Canyon Lake is an impoundment on the Guadalupe River, beginning about 12 miles northwest of New Braunfels. The dam, completed in 1964, provides an important water source for nearby municipalities and industries as well as power generation and flood control. The reservoir, operated by the Guadalupe–Blanco River Authority and maintained by the U.S. Army Corps of Engineers, has a storage capacity of 386,200 acre-feet.

Beyond its main purpose, the 8,240 surface acres of Canyon Lake's sparkling waters and its 60 miles of rocky shoreline offer relaxation and recreation to a wide area, with camping, fishing, and boating. Sailing is especially popular, and many sailors come from the nearest large city, San Antonio.

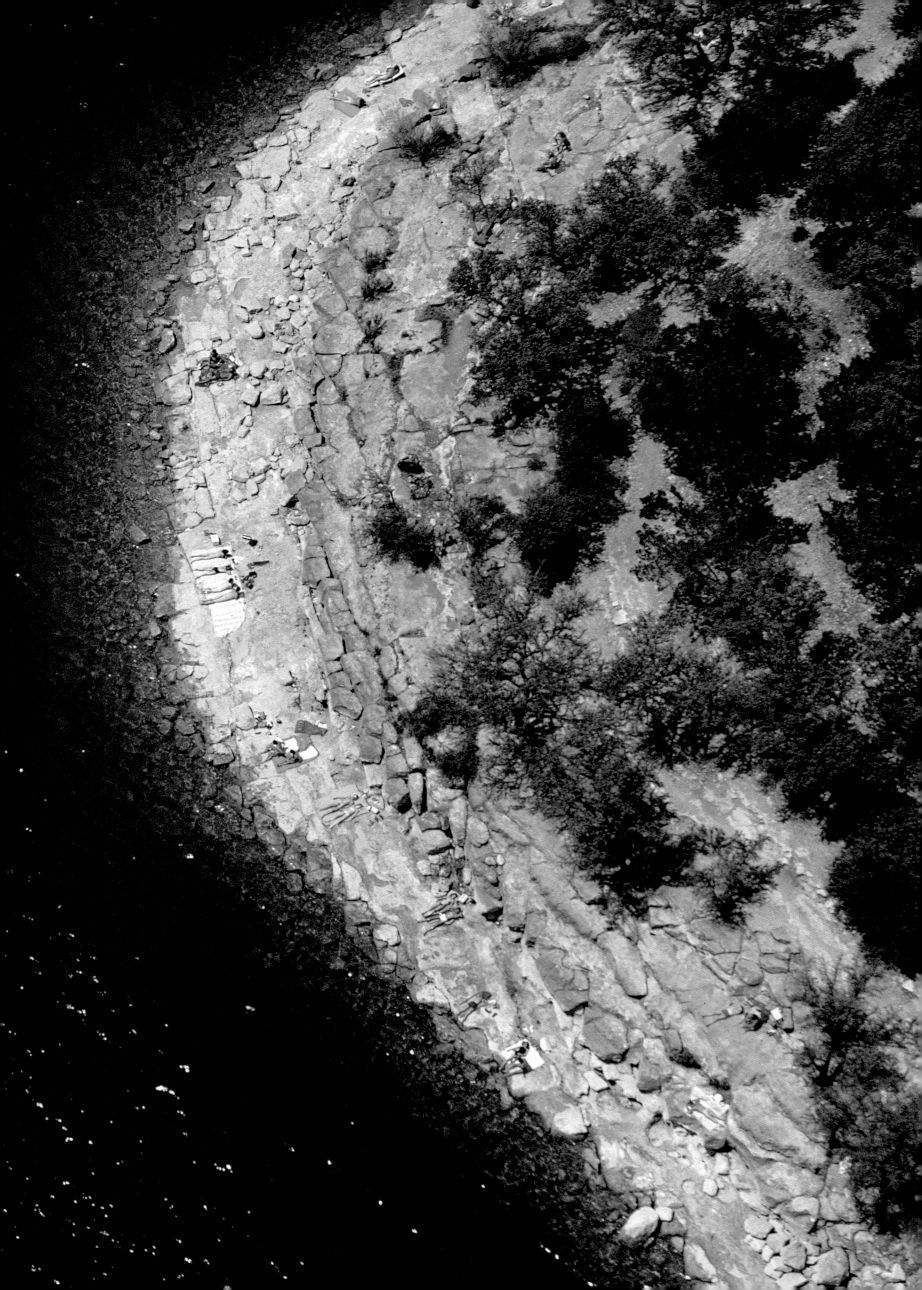

Lake Travis, Travis and Burnet Counties: In 1934 Mansfield Dam was built on an old crossing of the Colorado River some 20 miles northwest of Austin, creating Lake Travis. Since then a series of man-made lakes called the Highland Lakes region, has been constructed. These dams and reservoirs provide flood control, irrigation for farmers and ranchers, electrical power and last but hardly least, scenic beauty and recreation.

Lake Travis extends for about 65 miles up the Colorado River. Drawing from both Austin and San Antonio to the south, many areas bordering the water have been extensively developed with summer or retirement homes, resorts and planned residential communities. Because of the mild climate, sailboating and fishing are year-round pastimes.

TONY WEISSGARBER

The LBJ Ranch on the Pedernales River near Stonewall: President Lyndon Baines Johnson's home place is now two parks: the Lyndon B. Johnson National Historic Park and the Lyndon B. Johnson State Historic Park, preserved in honor of the first Texan to reach the nation's highest office. Both are on Ranch Road No. 1 off Highway 290 at Stonewall, between Johnson City and Fredericksburg.

The state park has a visitor center complete with exhibits and film shows, a nature trail with audio stations, a swimming pool, lighted tennis courts, baseball diamond, a recreation building, and picnic sites. The Sauer-Beckmann farmstead features living history demonstrations of Hill Country life. Small herds of buffalo, longhorn cattle, and white-tail deer also graze in the park.

The national park is accessible only by bus tours that originate in the state park. Across the river, this property includes the Johnson home, the Texas White House between 1964-8, and ranch outbuildings, the Johnson homestead where the president was born, the Junction School he attended as a child, and the LBJ gravesite. Both parks are open daily except Christmas.

The LBJ Ranch lies in the Hill Country, a large region in the center of the state. The Pedernales River (which would be called a creek anywhere but Central Texas) rises in Gillespie County and flows into the Colorado
Continued overleaf

River above Austin, flowing about 100 miles. The underlying land is a large limestone plateau, the fringes of the North American Great Plains that disappear at the Balcones Fault. Over the millenia small streams have carved canyons through the hills; the aspect, especially to the west, is mountainous, although the elevations are low, rising no more than 2,500 feet. The hills are studded with cedars and oaks, and native pecan trees spread through the bottoms. The soils are usually thin and rocky (Pedernales means "flinty" in Spanish), producing only a few good brown-earth meadows. The water is normally clear and fast, slicing over brown limestone and beds of watercress between more sluggish, milky pools. Tall cypress trees and fragrant sycamores shade the streams. The air is light and clear, blue sky by day and brilliant, low-hung stars by night.

The climate is mild. In spring, bluebonnets, the state flower, splash pool-like across the meadows, speckled with other red and yellow wildflowers. By summer the grasses turn brown, and the live oaks turn ocher in the fall. This is some of the most scenic country in Texas. For generations it was the southernmost hunting ground of the Penateka Comanches. The area was rich in game. The buffalo halted here, deterred by the heat below the Scarp, and there were wild turkey, bear, and white-tail deer. The bison, bear, and the big cats have disappeared, but deer are plentiful. Hunting brings thousands of visitors in the fall. The game the Indians scorned, such as rabbits and squirrels, are so numerous they are classed as varmints with no closed season. However, like most hard but scenic regions, this has always been a difficult place to make a living. Most of the land cannot be farmed. Rainfall is not dependable; neither is the grass. Most of the land is left for grazing cattle, sheep, and goats.

The first settlers to put permanent roots in this land were German immigrants in the 1840s. They made a treaty with the Comanches and staked out fields, building the town of Fredericksburg on the Pedernales. They were joined by English-speaking migrants out of Alabama and Tennessee. The two peoples merged but never quite absorbed each other. Later, Mexican workers came up from the south. The region has retained all those influences.

This was true pioneer country, and it has kept much of the flavor. Even until the 1940s there were few paved roads connecting the scattered small ranches and farms. The towns are still quite small. More and more, however, the natural beauty of the land, the cool hills and clear water and splendid all-year climate have made the Hill Country desirable for resort and retirement homes. Valleys along the streams where a man could not make a living raising oats or goats bring high prices from city folks.

Brenham, Washington County: This is country steeped in the Texas past. Washington-on-the-Brazos, near the confluence of the Brazos and Navasota Rivers a few miles away, was the site of the signing of the Texas Declaration of Independence, on March 2, 1836. This was one of the areas first settled by Anglo colonists, and Washington County was organized in 1837 under the laws of the republic. The Brazos settlement had another brief fling with glory between 1842–4, when government records were stored there while the cities of Austin and Houston engaged in the so-called "Archives War." Austin won and remained the capital. Brenham (named for a Texas soldier of fortune who had the bad luck to draw a black bean at Mier) was voted the county seat in 1844, and Washington-on-the-Brazos was relegated to a historic relic.
In antebellum times the Brazos bottomlands were rich cotton-plantation country. Fine homes were built in Brenham, some of which still stand. The town and area played an important role in educational and religious development. Texas' first institution of higher learning, Independence Academy for Women, was founded in 1837; other important universities, which later moved, began here. Although there were no large towns, Washington County was the most populous in Texas through the 1870s.
Between 1867–9 many German settlers moved in, and the economy of the county changed from cotton plantations to small farms. Today there are about 22,000 people in the county, half of them living in Brenham and there is manufacturing and some oil. Ninety percent of the agricultural income now comes from cattle, hogs, horses, dairy products, and poultry. A cotton plantation or farm is not to be found.

GEORGE HALL

TONY WEISSGARBER

Fort Hood: Military traditions of all kinds run deep in Texas. In the early years of statehood two-thirds of the U.S. Army was stationed on the Texas frontier, and when the Indian wars subsided, a climate suitable for year-round training and flying, the availability of open terrain, the attitude of the people — in some cases citizens and communities purchased land for military bases and donated it to the government — and the adroit footwork of Texas politicians all combined to maintain a large and lasting military presence in the state. Fort Hood, in Coryell and Bell Counties in Central Texas, holds the largest concentration of armored power in the United States and the biggest population of any military post in the Free World. The fort was activated in 1942 as part of the war effort, designated a permanent installation in 1950. It normally houses two armored divisions with a host of smaller units and support troops, supporting some 160,000 active and retired soldiers, dependents, and civilians, with a monthly military payroll of about $35 million.

Killeen, at the main entrance to Fort Hood, was a village of some 600 in 1950. In 1980 it had grown to 46,296 and become part of a metropolitan area of 157,820, an expansion that shows no signs of halting.

Visitors are generally welcome, and special activities for the public are held on occasions such as July 4 and Armed Forces Day.

East Texas and the Piney Woods

Davy Crockett National Forest, Houston County: Texans call deep East Texas the Piney Woods. This is a different world from the rest of Texas. Here the rain falls more than 50 inches a year and has created a forested region that runs 75 to 125 miles westward from the Louisiana border, ending in the post oak belt; and south from the Red River to about 25 miles from the Gulf of Mexico, enclosing an area of 16 million acres. This is an extension of the Southern forest into Texas, and it is also an extension — cultural as well as topographical — of the Deep South across the Texas line.

The forests are mostly pine, with three native trees — longleaf, shortleaf and loblolly pines — predominating. The slash pine has been extensively used in replantings. However, there are also significant stands of hardwoods — oak, elm, hickory, magnolia, sweet and black gum, and tupelo — among the numerous stream beds and river valleys.

Davy Crockett National Forest, named for the Alamo hero, is one of four national forests in the state, all in East Texas. It covers 161,493 acres in Houston and Trinity Counties.

BILL ELLZEY

Left

Kennard Sawmill, Davy Crockett National Forest: Virtually all of Texas' large commercial timber production comes from the Piney Woods, a territory bigger than the states of Massachusetts and Vermont combined. The 11.5 million acres of forest lands have an estimated timber value of $6.3 billion, and many loggers believe that the future of forestry in the United States lies in the Southern woods, especially as the Pacific Northwest timberlands become exhausted.

Sawlog production in East Texas declined in the early 1980s due to economic conditions, but in 1981 the 863.7 million board feet sold was part of a total harvest that brought in $502 million.

Above

Sam Houston National Forest, near Huntsville: Named for the victor of the battle at San Jacinto (and also Texas president, U.S. senator, and state governor), Sam Houston National Forest sprawls across Montgomery, Walker and San Jacinto Counties on the southern edge of the Piney Woods. Like all national forests in Texas, it offers recreation; and since these 160,000 beautiful acres are close to the city of Houston, the forest has become a major relaxation spot.

Six different areas within the park provide camping, picnicking, fishing, swimming and boating. The Lone Star Hiking Trail traverses the forest. While food is available from concessions, other facilities such as toilets and shelter are primitive.

Sunset over Sam Rayburn Reservoir: If half of Texas has too little water, the Piney Woods suffers from an embarrassment of riches. The Neches River in East Texas drains an area of 10,000 square miles and pours an annual 6 million acre-feet of water into the Gulf of Mexico. To save some of this flow for flood control, power generation, recreation and all the usual uses, the McGee Bend Dam was placed on the Angelina, the principal tributary of the Neches River, in Jasper County. The project was started in the 1950s; the name was changed in 1963 to honor Sam Rayburn, the late, great, longtime Speaker of the U.S. House of Representatives from Bonham. When impoundment was begun in 1965, water backed up through five East Texas counties: Jasper, Angelina, Sabine, San Augustine and Nacogdoches.

BILL ELLZEY

The Sam Rayburn reservoir is an impounded river that winds through the woods, covering 113,400 acres with a total capacity of 2,852,600 acre-feet. The two hydroelectric generating units at the dam have been producing energy since 1966. The facility is owned by the federal government and maintained by the U.S. Army Corps of Engineers.

The Piney Woods at winter sunset: Humidity from regular rainfall and vast quantities of surface water combines with smoke to create the hazy sky.

BILL ELLZEY

Country store in the Piney Woods: The general store, which sold everything from canned goods to ladies' fashions and from firearms to fertilizer, is no longer a fixture of rural Texas as it was until the 1940s. The movement of people to town and city and the coming of good paved roads, even in the remote areas of the state, caused most isolated rural stores to disappear. They have, of course, reappeared in a fashion in the city convenience store.

Some store locations sprouted into towns; some have been abandoned. But some, with a gas pump added in the 1920s, still survive. These are no longer "general" stores, offering a bit of everything, but carry items that someone may need but which aren't worth the long drive to town. Large parts of the Piney Woods are really more remote, locked in the trees, than the unpopulated expanses of West Texas — and here the friendly crossroads store remains.

BILL ELLZEY

Tyler, Rose Capital of the World: Tyler, named for the tenth president of the United States, was founded in 1846 but only achieved city status in 1907. The great East Texas oil discoveries in 1931 in Smith and nearby counties did not plant derricks in the streets, as at Kilgore, but they did bring the whole country out of the backwoods. Today, diversified manufacturing creates more income in Smith County than oil and agribusiness together.

Tyler, however, is known for roses. The sweetest roses this side of England thrive in the mild climate and sandy soil. Half the entire U.S. production of rosebushes comes from a 15-mile radius around the city. Twenty million, worth $70 million to the local economy, are shipped each year. Tyler holds a Rose Festival annually, and the city maintains a 22-acre rose garden, exhibiting 38,000 bushes and 400 varieties. Roses grow here among pine trees, fountains, gazebos, archways and pools.

BILL ELLZEY

BILL ELLZEY

Right

La Gloria Refinery, Tyler: Beyond the money derived from the export and sale of oil and gas, mineral wealth has created a great infrastructure of petroleum industries in East Texas. Refineries, cracking plants and petrochemical industries have proliferated. If 20,000 East Texans are employed in oil and gas extraction, another 30,000 work in oil-supply and oil- and gas-related enterprises. East Texas now produces only about 12 percent of the oil in the state, but cities like Tyler and nearby Longview — the service center of the petroleum industry — have found significant secondary and tertiary sources of wealth.

Pine logging camp, Sabine County: The Texas lumber and wood products industry provides employment for some 41,000 people; 8,000 are engaged in logging. After the bad old "cut and run" days, when forests were felled with no thought of reseeding and replenishment of this renewable source, Texas loggers had a good record of conservation for 50 years. During the boom of the late 1970s, however, more trees were cut than planted — a trend that worries conservationists and which the lumber industry understands cannot continue.

While Texas has 23.4 million acres of woodlands, only the pine–hardwood forests of the east figure in the commercial future and the key to the Southern forests' future will be successful management and renewal.

BILL ELLZEY

Rural cemetery, East Texas: In 1940 Texas was predominantly rural, though today 80 percent of the people live in urban areas. Reminders of this once-heavy farming population are found in the country cemeteries — some still in use, some not, and some on private land — which are part of the heritage of this land. The pine forests were among the earliest settled parts of the state; there were Anglo-Saxon squatters here even before the Spanish government authorized American colonization. But since 1900 two-thirds of all Texas counties have steadily lost population.

All across the eastern half of the state many old cemeteries, mostly well-tended, remain where there is no human habitation for miles. Signs on highways sometimes point these out because they are historic sites in their own right.

These lonely spots record Texas' recent past as faithfully as the more resplendent tombs of Rome, and records of them are maintained.

Nacogdoches: Named for a vanished tribe of Caddoan Indians, Nacogdoches was one of three successful Spanish settlements in Texas before the arrival of American colonists. It is the oldest city in the state. La Salle came here in 1687, causing the Spanish to place a mission among the Indians. After various efforts, this was abandoned in 1762; however, in 1779 Spanish settlers under Gil Ybarbo moved here, deep in the forest, to avoid the Comanches on the plains. Because of the proximity of the Louisiana border, they soon established a lucrative smuggling trade.

BILL ELLZEY

Ybarbo built a stone warehouse to store his goods and this became known as the Old Stone Fort. Though moved, the fort has been preserved. This building and Nacogdoches figured in every conspiracy, filibuster and rebellion that rocked early Texas. Spanish Royalists almost destroyed the town; the succeeding Mexican government stationed soldiers here. The first two Texan newspapers, *La Gaceta de Tejas* and *El Mejicano,* were published here, both begun in 1813. This history is celebrated in five local museums and there are 50 historical markers scattered through the town.

Today, Nacogdoches is mainly an agribusiness center — cattle, hogs, poultry and hay — with significant timbering and manufacturing. One of the most important enterprises is the university (above), called variously Stephen F. Austin Teacher's College, Stephen F. Austin State College and now Stephen F. Austin State University. After many efforts, it opened in 1923 and now enrolls about 12,000 students.

The Upper Gulf Coast Region

In 1892 a newcomer to Houston described it as "an insignificant town, malodorous bayou, and intolerable mud."

Today the mud is gone, replaced by endless paving (which causes floods). The industrial areas and ship channel can be malodorous indeed but Houston is anything but insignificant. There are more than 1.6 million people within the city limits and the surrounding metropolitan area has a population exceeding 3 million. Houston is the metropolis of Texas, the second port and the fifth-largest city in the United States. And the Gulf coastal region, which it dominates, is becoming the Third Coast in more than Texas brag.

This coastal prairie, which runs westward from the Sabine River and Louisiana boundary and inland between 30–60 miles, is a grassy plain cut by numerous swampy, brushy streams called bayous. For centuries Europeans avoided it; it was hot, humid, unhealthy and the home of Karankawa Indians, noted mainly for ritual cannibalism. The French explorer La Salle did establish a fort here, but that came to a bad end.

However, when American colonists began to arrive in 1822 the rich muck of the heavy alluvial soils quickly attracted cotton planters. The Brazos River bottoms drew most of the settlers and got the glory, but Southern planters with black slaves appropriated much of the prairies. And Buffalo Bayou, debouching into Galveston Bay, was seen as a strategic waterway from the inland cotton plantations to the Gulf. A trading post at the junction of Bray's and Buffalo Bayous soon became the town of Harrisburg, important in the 1830s.

Immediately after Texan independence was won at nearby San Jacinto, two Yankee promoters, the Allen brothers, unable to acquire land around Harrisburg, pushed some 50 miles inland up the narrow, brushy creek, finding what they believed was its true limit of navigation. Here they announced the town of Houston, offering lots for $50 with easy credit. John Allen, as a member of the Texas Congress, politicked — with offers of free land and credits — the Republic into designating Houston the capital.

This was characteristic of Houston's future: it was situated where things could happen, but men had to make them happen.

The capital was soon lost to Austin, but a start had been made. In 1837 the Allens paid to have the steamship *Laura* sail up the bayou to prove their point. The passage was not auspicious; passengers had to remove sunken logs and clear overhanging branches from the way, and the ship almost sailed past "Houston," which consisted of some surveyors' stakes, a tent, and human footprints on the muddy bank. Still, the point was made.

Before the Civil War, Houston secured the first railroad, giving it a dominant edge over rival shipping points along the coast. Then, in the 1870s, the bayou was dredged to a depth of 12 feet and a pass cut through Redfish Bar, a reef in the bay that had blocked entry from the sea. Houstonians received a little money from Congress and the aid of the U.S. Corps of Engineers for this project. Now, the channel was the only dependable waterway to the principal port at Galveston and Houston became the center of the cotton trade.

When Spindletop, Texas' first gusher, blew in in 1901 with both rails and waterway Houston was ready to reap. The final obstacle was overcome with the creation of a deep channel, giving the port of Houston direct access to sea-going vessels. It took 50 years of dreaming and working to achieve this goal, but in 1910 residents devised the "Houston Plan," by which both the city and the federal government shared the cost. This was unprecedented at the time; Houston pioneered the plan, which became the basis for all future local government–federal financial cooperation. And it was also characteristic of the frontier spirit: Texans have never been against government intervention when government provides assistance without trying to tell Texans what to do.

By 1922 Houston was the largest cotton port in the world. It took only the discovery of the East Texas Field in 1931 to replace waning cotton tonnage with oil. With the coming of World War II Houston became the heart of the greatest concentration of petrochemical industry on Earth.

GEORGE HALL

Right Houston home: Conspicuous consumption in housing is alive and thriving in Houston as well as Dallas. The Third Coast may never rival the Hudson River valley for entrepreneurial mansions; the modern villas are put up with less medieval mysticism and servants are harder to come by than in the salad days of Newport. But the pool — essential in this climate — is no problem; pool services are contracted out.

River Oaks Country Club: The country club is a peculiarly American institution, denounced by populist politicians but seen by most people as a visible symbol of success. Texans' ceaseless drive for money and success, a battle in which only a few succeed, is probably no more marked than that of Americans on the other two coasts, but Texans are more open about it — and Texans more openly respect those who succeed. In a society without defined social ranks, the country club is a useful symbol of achieved status; only incidentally is it a place where businessmen play golf. The old social hierarchy of prestige — cotton money, oldest and therefore more acceptable; cattle money, newer and a bit uncouth; oil money, most nouveaux of the riches — has become much blurred; there is also new corporate money. Some "Oaks" are harder to join than others, but in a growing place like Texas time takes care of that.

Houston is a new city. Long after its founding, it lagged behind Galveston and San Antonio; it came into its own when dreams and restless energy — and no little political skill — combined to connect some of the richest mineral earth with the sea.

Most of the older structures have long since been removed, either by fire or to make way for new ones. Houston has been the boom town of the century. It sprawls; there is no one downtown anymore, but several — clusters of towers miles apart on the flat horizon. There is no way between these clusters and the homes that spread through three counties and have reached the Brazos 40 miles away, except by auto. And despite the best-conceived freeways in the world, traffic can be horrendous, with cars moving for miles at a snail's pace.

In recent years Houston has become the first city in the world in the manufacture of petroleum equipment, chemical fertilizers, pesticides and oil and gas pipeline transmission. It ranks first in the United States in building permits and construction goes on regardless of boom or bust. And Houston is among the top cities in the nation in commercial bank deposits, wholesale business, retail sales and industrial payrolls. It ranks fifth in the manufacture of machinery, sixth in fabricated metals. It is a leading scientific research and engineering center. It processes or makes almost everything.

The Houston area has more than 3,600 manufacturing plants and 200 major corporations have moved here since 1970. One transfer involved 10,000 employees.

Houston is the nation's second-largest seaport and the largest wheat-exporting port; it services a large part of the Midwest as well as Texas. It is the second U.S. port in total value of foreign trade behind New York and the third in total tonnage. Petroleum, petroleum products, lumber, grain and cotton are the staples of its seagoing trade, for Houston serves most of Texas. In 1981, the port handled 100.96 million short tons.

Houston is the money capital of Texas. It has drawn more than 50 foreign bank offices, from Swiss to Japanese. It has 53 consular offices and nearly 30 foreign trade, investment and tourism branches. And it is the first place that Texas politicians, bent on state-wide races, come seeking funds.

Houston's business is clearly business, making money from big deals and small ones. But wealth brings, and demands, other things. There are 20 colleges and universities; Rice University and the University of Houston are nationally known institutions. The public school system is the seventh largest in the United States, watched closely for its pioneering trends.

Houston is also an exuberant cultural center, although the emphasis is upon consumption rather than creation. But wealth is the supporter of the arts and Houston has become repository of world-famed art collections.

Houston is vibrant, hustling, sprawling. It is uncompressed but congested. The headlong growth of the 1970s has slowed; no city could handle such an embarrassment of newcomers and businesses.

With growth came all the problems of the modern megacity: crime, pollution, water shortage, smog, traffic jams and deteriorating or inadequate services. Growth led to over-building. The turning of the ship channel into one of the major chemical complexes of the world created a waterway that could be set on fire and whose fumes could asphyxiate ships' crews. Buffalo Bayou will never again be what it was in the old days, when steamboats paddled beside tree-lined banks, or even in the early seaport era, when sport fishermen waved to passing ocean liners. But massive efforts at cleanup and beautification have improved Houston's water quality. When the wind blows a certain way the downtown towers are wreathed in acidic haze but it is unlikely the channel will catch fire these days.

Houston has always made things happen. However other Texans may see the city — and to some it almost seems a foreign country — few are willing to bet that the same human drive that created all these problems will not find a way to solve them.

Left   Houses and high-rises, Houston: Houston is widely known as the only American metropolis without a zoning code, a reflection of Houstonians' determination to let nothing stand in the way of business. The notion fits comfortably with Texans' libertarian instincts; there was no zoning on the old frontier. The fact is, however, that while office buildings sometimes overshadow rose gardens, the city's general patterns of development have been essentially no different from large cities with elaborate zoning laws — proof that the developer usually prevails.

Houston, Texas' cosmopolitan metropolis,
known from Singapore to Saudi Arabia.

Docked ship, Houston ship channel.

Loading sulphur, Houston ship channel: Natural sulphur is mined from native deposits found in the salt dome formations along the Gulf Coast; it is also extracted from sour natural gas and oil. Texas is a major producer for the world; 5 million metric tons were mined in 1980.

GEORGE HALL

Below

The Astrodome, Houston: The Astrodome, adjacent to the Astroworld amusement park, a fully air-conditioned, enclosed stadium, is a modern manifestation of the pioneer spirit. The great dome and Astroturf, developed because grass will not grow indoors, have since been emulated across the land. Houston's professional football and baseball teams (Oilers, Gamblers, Astros) play here. The annual Bluebonnet Bowl is a major collegiate sports event.

GEORGE HALL

GEORGE HALL

Rice fields near Katy: Katy is on the edge of Harris County, just west of Houston. Even in the environs of the mighty Houston industrial complex, agriculture has an important place. Houston's county produces fine cattle — one head per acre — plus hogs and poultry, and there are 50,000 acres of irrigated rice lands. Rice farming began on the Texas coast in 1850 with 110 acres, and it was once Texas' third most valuable crop. Much less land is used for rice now than in the 1950s, but the total yields are larger due to extensive mechanization. Texas rice, grown in 20 coastal counties, is sown, fertilized, and sprayed with insecticides and herbicides by airplane.

Average yields run from 4,500 to 5,000 hundredweight per acre; the total crop in 1982 was 22,214,000 cwt. Although Texas produces only a small portion of the world's rice, the state is a major exporter, selling to some 100 countries. Many buyers consider it the best.

Houston bus station: For some, the beginning
of a Texas dream; for others, its end.

Texas Medical Center, Houston: On 220 acres in the midst of the city, the Texas Medical Center contains 24 hospitals, medical schools and research laboratories. The idea was conceived by trustees of the M. D. Anderson Foundation in the 1940s. Its growth has come in spurts: 1949–55, 1959–60 and 1963–5. The M. D. Anderson Hospital and Tumor Institute is known worldwide for cancer treatment. The center treats 1.5 million patients each year; its renowned specialists such as Dr. Denton Cooley (St. Luke's) and Dr. Michael E. DeBakey (Methodist Hospital) have drawn the rich and famous to Houston, from the late Duke of Windsor to tycoons and Arabian monarchs. In all, there are 62 hospitals in Houston and it has emerged as a leading world health-science center.

Gilley's: On Spencer Highway as one leaves Houston, Gilley's Rodeo is what Texans call "kicker heaven." The parking lot is wall-to-wall with pickups; inside, jeans and longnecks (this is what Lone Star beer comes in) are *derigueur*. Owner Mickey Gilley, the country–western singer, performs here, along with other big-name entertainers. But Gilley is not a Texan and on most nights the cowboys and cowgirls trying the mechanical bulls are apt to be newcomers or from New York.
The movie "Urban Cowboy" made Gilley's world famous, along with Texas chic.

Right Houston Intercontinental Airport: Texas ranks only behind California in the number of enplaned passengers and Houston is certifiably behind Dallas in one respect — Dallas, on the east–west route, has more traffic. Like many larger cities, Houston has two major airports: Hobby, closer in, is the older; Intercontinental was built out on the prairie (until the metropolitan area ingested it) to handle international trade. Together, Houston's air terminals handle more than 7 million passengers annually and about a quarter million of these go or come from abroad.

Above All along the Texas coast condominiums with access to the bays are big business and very "in." Anyone who lives near water and can afford a boat, has and operates one. Small craft are manufactured in many places, both along the Gulf and in Austin, near the Highland Lakes. The height of luxury is to tie your boat up to your own dock.

Left The Lyndon B. Johnson Manned Space Flight Center: Although it is a city in itself, the Johnson Space Center is considered part of Houston. The first word spoken from the moon, calling the center, was "Houston." Actually, the complex is in southern Harris County about 25 miles from downtown Houston, on Clear Lake, an inlet of Galveston Bay. The site was donated by Rice University. All American space flights have been controlled from here since October 1962. The facility was established as part of NASA's lunar landing program in 1961. Criticism that Vice President

Lyndon Johnson of Texas and powerful local Congressman Albert Thomas secured the site for the Texas coast through political pressure has not survived the years; the choice met all requirements, from mid-continental southern location to nearby supporting high-tech and educational institutions. The center is open to the public, and space-flight history is exhibited daily.

GEORGE HALL

Above Houston ship channel. The Houston ship channel once wandered through 51 miles of prairie to the sea. Today the port area and the channel banks are solidly encrusted with refineries and every kind of petrochemical plant. The channel, constantly maintained and improved, can handle any shipping and is one of the busiest waterways in the world.

Left   San Jacinto Monument on Buffalo Bayou: On this site (though the actual battlefield is now under water because the bayou has shifted), Texas won its independence from Mexico on April 21 1836. Here, beside the Houston ship channel, Texas maintains a 445-acre park, with a reflecting pool, picnic grounds, great oaks, and grave markers. The monument, taller than the Washington Monument, is the result of a 1930s WPA project, an art deco shaft faced with Texas fossil-studded limestone. Visitors may take an elevator to the top to view the area.

Because of the growth of the ship channel, there is much development nearby. The park has become enclosed with the symbols of modern industrial Texas.

Above
The Battleship *Texas,* San Jacinto Battleground: The USS *Texas II,* known as the "Battleship *Texas,*" is moored in honorable retirement in a giant slip beside the battlefield. The *Texas* saw action in World War II from the Normandy beachhead to the Okinawa landings. For many years, as the result of a Gulf hurricane, she rested at a slight tilt.

The Big Thicket.

BILL ELLZEY

Deep in the wildwood: Church at Camp Ruby.

Big Thicket road.

BILL ELLZEY

The Big Thicket of Texas was just that in the early days: 3 million acres of impenetrable wilderness, a dense tangle of trees, brush, and swamp water between the Gulf and the East Texas pine forest. Lumbering and development have destroyed most of it this century, but its remote stretches remain places of beauty and horror, with four of the five carnivorous plants found in North America, 21 varieties of orchids and countless species of fungi in the dank woods. Alligators and bald eagles survive, although the spectacular ivory-billed woodpecker has been lost.

Because of the unique ecology of the Big Thicket there has been a long battle between preservationists and lumber and development interests. In the 1960s it was vanishing at the rate of 50 acres a day. In 1974, the Big Thicket National Preserve was authorized by Congress to set aside 84,550 acres in Orange, Jefferson, Liberty and adjacent counties. Of twelve proposed units, to date, only three have been completed: Turkey Creek, Beech Creek and Hickory Creek Savannah. These, with several waterways, are open to the public.

BILL ELLZEY

THE UPPER GULF COAST REGION ☆ 227

Offshore oil rig near Galveston: The petroleum deposits that lie under Texas extend far out into Gulf waters. Under Spanish law, to which the U.S. Supreme Court agreed, mineral rights accrued to Texas, not the federal government. An enormous controversy over this was decided in the 1950s in favor of Texas, and President Eisenhower's backing Texas was a major factor in his carrying the state over the Democratic candidate, who took the other position. The tidelands subsequently have added enormous revenues to the state treasury.

Most production comes from between the three-mile line and the three marine-league line, in relatively shallow water. Offshore rigs are worked from platforms that are towed to the site and supported by legs jacked down to the bottom.

BILL ELZEY

Galveston: The first community on Galveston island, named for the Spanish general who assisted the American cause by fighting the British in the Gulf during the Revolution, was founded by Jean Lafitte, the pirate. But the sheltered bay soon made Galveston the chief port for all Texas and its largest town by 1838. Texas' first convent, bank and chamber of commerce were organized here. Nineteenth-century prosperity resulted in a plethora of fine Victorian houses, many of which, with the Strand or old dockside district, have been restored.

Galveston was seized by the Federal Army in 1862 during the Civil War but it was quickly recaptured by the Confederates. The deadly tidal wave of 1900, which cost 5,000–7,000 lives, did not destroy its grandeur, but the seaport, which shipped 11 million short tons in 1981, was transcended by Houston and Texas City once the ship channel was completed. Today Galveston is known principally as a seaside resort, with hotels, piers and nightclubs. Servicing offshore oil drilling is also important.

Barge in Galveston Bay: Canals have been dredged through Texas bays, creating a coastal system of inland waterways that supports heavy barge traffic from the tip of the state to the Louisiana border.

Right and below

Houses, Galveston Island, Jamaica Beach: Despite the perennial warnings of experts about the hazards of the hurricane coast and frequent damaging storms (the last one hit Galveston Island in 1983), Texans flock to Gulf beaches and islands, which have become some of the hottest resort properties anywhere. Houses are often built on piles as a concession to rising waters. But nothing can overcome the allure of having a home at the beach or a condominium in some planned seaside development, with one's private boat dock, as here at Jamaica Beach, a town of about 350 on the west end of Galveston Island.

BILL ELLZEY

Beach, Galveston.

Below

Snow geese, Anahuac National Wildlife Refuge: In Chambers County on the upper Gulf coast, the refuge was established in 1963 as a wintering place for four species of geese and other waterfowl, and a year-round home for mottled ducks. Altogether there are 253 species of birds on the refuge checklist, of which 42 nest here. The once-threatened American alligator has also found a haven at Anahuac.

Snow geese *(Chen caerulescens)* are called both snow and blue geese; the colors are merely different feather stages of the same bird. They winter in Texas in huge numbers and are not an endangered species.

The Coastal Bend

The sun and sea meet in the middle of Texas' 624 miles of coastline at the Coastal Bend.

This shoreline does not face upon the open Gulf. The surf breaks upon the clean beaches on a tier of long, narrow barrier islands standing a few miles offshore, low strips of sand that shelter an indented coastline of bays, inlets, peninsulas, and tidal marshes. It is a topography that provides bright beaches accessible by causeway on the islands, calm green bays, and flats teeming with fish and waterfowl.

The barrier islands are geologically very new; they were thrown up by surf action no more than 4,000 years ago. They are still evolving: almost entirely sand with unstable vegetation, they accrete here, wash away shoreline there, always subject to the pressures of wind and water. The shallower cuts and passes that open the bays to the Gulf regularly silt up in places that are not maintained by dredging, only to be reopened by periodic storms.

Reefs form across the mouths of Texas rivers flowing into the Gulf; historically this has made them impassable to large, sea-going ships. The early Texas seaports were situated in bays, like Galveston, until modern ship channels were dredged in this century. And some bayside ports are still important, because of the creation of the Intracoastal Waterway.

Although Spanish galleons sailed the Texas coast from the early 1500s — and some were wrecked there — the tidal shoreline was explored and mapped relatively late in colonial history. Although captain Joaquin Orobio y Basterta sailed Corpus Christi Bay in 1747, naming it for the Archangel Michael, the Coastal Bend was not surveyed until 1766, when Colonel Diego Ortiz de Parilla led an expedition from La Bahia to the mouth of the Rio Grande. Parilla traversed and named Copano and Corpus Christi Bays, Matagorda, Mustang, and San Jose Islands.

Copano Bay, the closest point on water with access to the Gulf from La Bahia and San Antonio, became the major shipping station for south-central Texas for many years. It figured in the settlement of Texas and in the war for independence in 1836. Fannin's hapless army landed here, and in 1836 after San Jacinto, Texas "horse marines" — actually mounted Rangers — captured three Mexican ships by stratagem in Copano Bay. Today, while the Intracoastal Canal traverses the outer bays, they have been superseded by the man-made port at Corpus Christi, the third-busiest in Texas.

Back from the bays the Coastal Bend is a continuation of the Gulf prairie that follows the whole shoreline. The soils are alluvial, mainly sandy loams excellent for growing grains. There is less rainfall here than on the upper Gulf, grasses are shorter, and the small timbers mostly live oaks and mesquites. But this is still good grazing land, and the ubiquitous petroleum deposits have been found all along the coast.

Petroleum, cattle, and farming all blend well here as in other parts of the state, and they create an infrastructure of industries based on petrochemicals and the processing of agricultural and sea products. Grain sorghums are Corpus Christi's major export; the surrounding Coastal Bend grows more sorghums than any other part of Texas. And there are shipbuilding, oil servicing, and aluminum industries.

However, the coast is sun and sea, attractive to man since the race began, and the coastal regions of America are the fastest-growing in the nation. The middle Texas coast has surf and sand and cool Gulf breezes, drawing tourists and summer residents. Commercial fishing is significant, but the real action on most of the coast is in recreation, whether fishing or boating in the bays, pursuing billfish offshore, or simply lazing in the sun. All are possible for a large part of the year.

This is a storm-lashed coast, subject to periodic tropical hurricanes. Cabeza de Vaca was the first European shipwrecked here. Since then there has been enormous destruction of property and in the old days, before weather advisories and warning systems, there was much loss of life. But once storms have passed the coast is quickly rebuilt. Just as men have always gone down to the sea in ships whatever the perils, so long as there is a Third Coast Texans will inhabit and enjoy it.

Sailing on Texas' Third Coast: Catamaran on Corpus Christi Bay.

Padre Island: Dreams of seashells and pirate treasure.

Below
Padre Island, with Laguna Madre in the background.

Padre is the best known of the Texas barrier islands. The northern end is accessible by causeway from Corpus Christi, and South Padre from Port Isabel. Padre Island is actually connected to Mustang Island when the pass between them is closed. From there it runs south 110 miles, ending at Brazos de Santiago Pass, a few miles above the Rio Grande.

The island was named for Padre Nicolas Balli, who received it as a grant from the Spanish crown about 1800. Long abandoned, until recent times remote and accessible only by boat, it has a colorful history of lonely ranching families and great houses destroyed by storms and legends — some of them true — of Indians, pirates, and sunken Spanish treasure. It is a favorite haunt for beachcombers and underwater salvors, and a battleground for treasure seekers and archaeologists.

Both the northern and southern tips have been developed for tourism with hotels, condominiums, and marinas; South Padre Island has emerged as a major year-round resort. However, an 80-mile-long section was made into the Padre Island National Seashore in 1968 — the only such national park — in order to preserve the unspoiled beauty of its dunes and beaches and fragile island ecology.

GEORGE HALL

Right

The High Bridge, Corpus Christi: This soars over the ship channel; the port of Corpus Christi lies just behind. The harbor was completed in 1926, and it was designed for both beauty and utility by the artist Gutzon Borglum, who also created Mt. Rushmore.

Corpus Christi, city on the sea: On Corpus Christi Bay, this is one of the loveliest cities in this or any other state. It is a major port with a diversified economy including agriculture, oil, manufacturing, and military bases supporting a metropolitan population of about 330,000. But it is also a splendid resort area for both Texans and northern visitors. Busy shoreline boulevards run between the seawall and houses, apartments, offices, and hotels. A famous feature of the city are the T-head piers, reserved for tour and fishing boats and small pleasure craft, which jut from the center of town into the bay.

Below
Tugboats, Corpus Christi harbor.

BILL ELLZEY

Sun and sea: Sunset over the tidal flats of
Redfish Bay, near Aransas Pass.

Church of Nuestra Señora del Espiritú Santo de Zuñiga, Goliad.

Above After being moved several times, the Spanish mission of Nuestra Señora del Espiritú Santo de Zuñiga was established on the San Antonio River in 1749 to christianize the Karankawa Indians. The Presidio or Fort of Nuestra Señora de Loreto was erected to protect the friars. Unfortunately, more European smallpox than religion was transmitted to the tribe. While the mission failed, a small community grew up about the fort, which came to be called La Bahia. The old presidio retained the name, although the town, one of three surviving Spanish settlements in Texas, was renamed Goliad (an acronym of Hidalgo, the Mexican revolutionary hero) in 1829. The old fortress was the scene of many battles during the turbulent early nineteenth century. Colonel Fannin and his men were massacred here in 1836 after surrendering to the Mexican Army. Church services have been held continuously in the chapel since 1840, but the presidio itself fell into ruin. Beginning in 1968 it was restored to former and present splendor by the Kathryn O'Connor Foundation and is a National Historic Landmark.

BILL ELLZEY

Wintering flocks, Aransas National Wildlife Refuge.

Below
Shorebirds, Aransas National Wildlife Refuge.

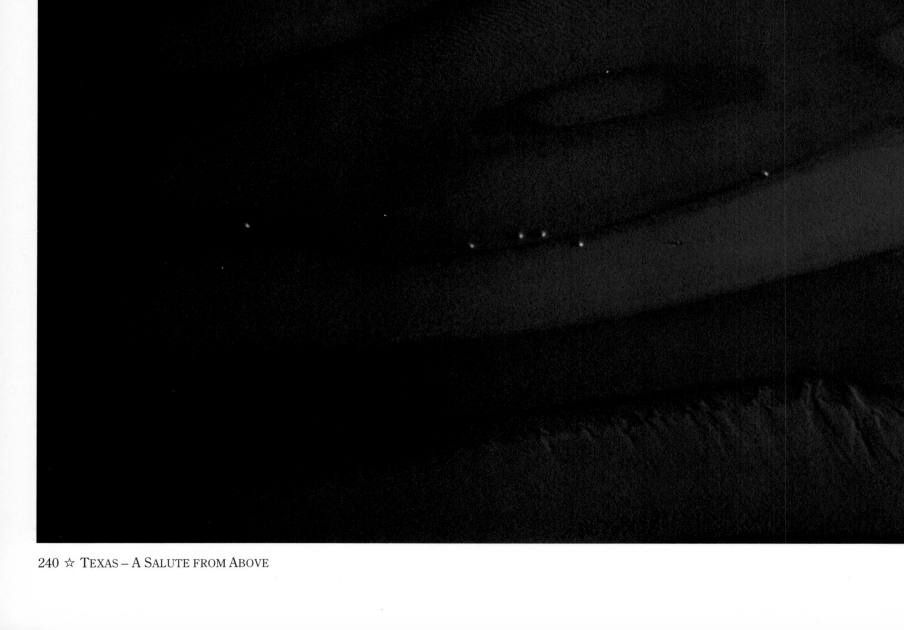

BILL ELLZEY

Observation platform for viewing whooping cranes.

Texas is one of the great remaining repositories of wildlife in the nation. While most of this wildlife is found on private lands, which may be hunted, the federal government maintains 10 national refuges in Texas totalling 177,500 acres. The state has set aside 19 wildlife management areas. The Aransas National Wildlife Refuge was established in 1937 as a wintering sanctuary for waterfowl and wading birds. It has become nationally known as the refuge for the whooping crane, a magnificent migratory bird whose numbers have long teetered on the edge of extinction. More than 350 species of bird life have been cataloged here, as well as many mammals such as deer and raccoons. Annual archery deer hunting is held, however, to prevent overpopulation. The refuge is open to bird watchers; the best months are November through March when most waterfowl and the prized whoopers are present.

Key Allegro, Rockport.

BILL ELLZEY

The pretty coastal village of Rockport (permanent population about 3,500) is on Live Oak Peninsula between Copano and Aransas Bays, facing Aransas Bay. The beach is sheltered from the Gulf by San José (or St. Joseph) Island. This was a shipping point for cowhides and tallow after the Civil War, soon sporting a wharf and hotel and reaching a population of 1,500 by 1890. Bypassed by the ports of Aransas Pass and Corpus Christi long ago, the Rockport area turned to tourism and recreation. Fishing is important and the Texas State Marine Biology Lab is here. But Rockport, nearby Fulton, and the peninsula generally now depend on hunting and fishing, which draw people from a wide area.
Long ago many splendid summer homes were built along the bay. Key Allegro, a Venice-like resort on the water and connected to Rockport by a short causeway, is typical of more modern developments that give immediate access to the all-important sea.

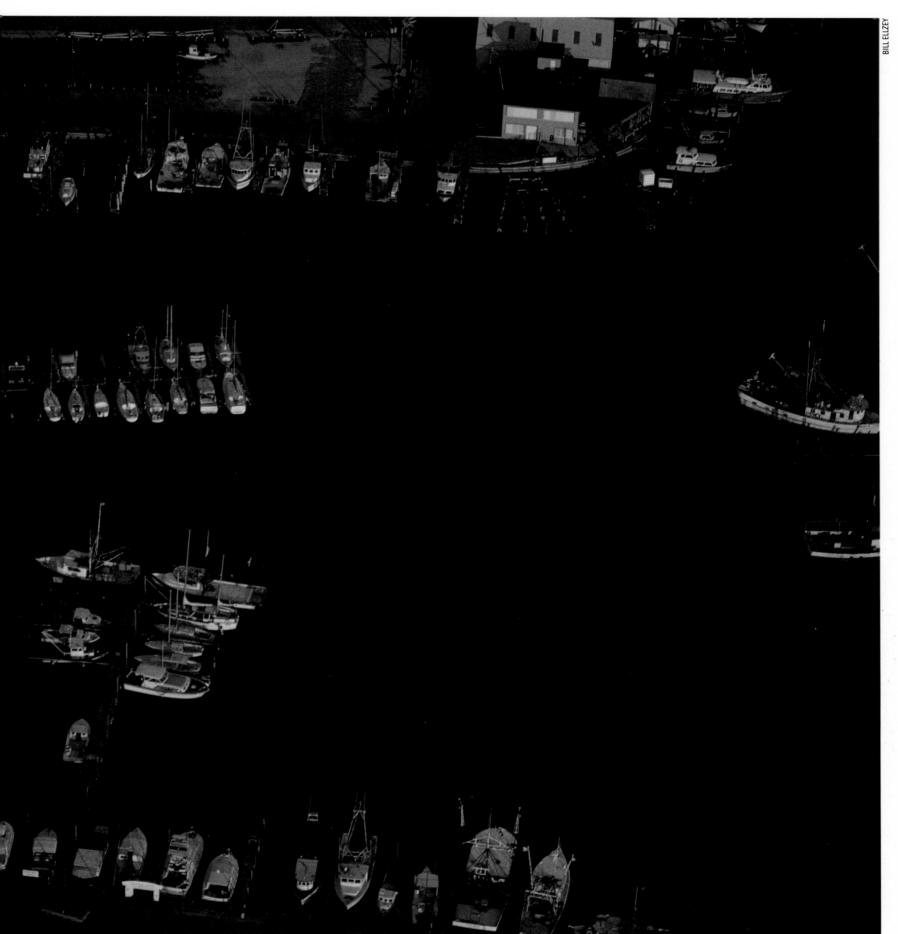

Pleasure boats, Key Allegro.

BILL ELLZEY

Aluminum plant near Aransas Pass.

Port Aransas: Aransas Pass and Port Aransas (the name is derived from Aranzazu, a Spanish palace) can confuse even Texans. The former is a town of about 7,000 on the mainland lying partly in each of Aransas, Nueces, and San Patricio Counties. It is a deepwater port on the Intracoastal Canal, and oil production, refining, shipbuilding, and manufacturing, as well as fishing and shrimping, are all important. Port Aransas, however, is on Mustang Island across Redfish and Corpus Christi Bays, connected by a causeway with Aransas Pass. It was known as Tarpon until 1911. Although

this town of 2,000 is built beside the deepwater channel that joins the port of Corpus Christi with the Gulf, and ocean-going traffic passes this way, it is not, despite the name, primarily a seaport. Port Aransas is a fishing resort. Both aluminum and shipbuilding are significant industries in the Coastal Bend; one of the major imports at Corpus Christi is bauxite or aluminum ore. And it should surprise no one that the principal business of many Texas shipyards is the fabrication or repair of offshore oil equipment.

Below Corpus Christi waste treatment plant.

South Texas

South Texas begins at San Antonio and runs south between the Gulf of Mexico and the Rio Grande, forming a great triangle on the map. Because of its very different climate and ecology, however, the tip of this triangle is usually designated as the Lower Rio Grande Valley.

This South Texas region is sometimes called the Rio Grande Plain, 20 million acres of subtropical dry-land vegetation including such exotic wild shrubs as prickly pear, cactus, mesquite, catclaw, dwarf oak, huisache, and cenizo, which grow together to make thickets in many places. This is also known as the Brush Country, or in Spanish, the *monte* or the *chaparral*. Another name is *brasada,* referring to a land baked under a blazing sun.

It was once a vast savannah with rich grasses interspersed only with clumps of mesquites and oaks. Here the Spanish and Mexicans introduced the cattle culture that grew up in Mexico, complete with cattle brands, horsemen's costume, semi-feudal social relationships between hand and brand, and the working jargon of the cow country. Mustang, lariat, buckaroo come from *mesteño, la reata, vaquero.* From here, Texans exploded both the cattle and the culture across all the Western states.

Millions of half-wild longhorns roamed this country after the Civil War, before over-grazing led to the rapid spread of cactus and brush. It is still cattle, sheep, and goat country, though oil and gas fields are also cultivated. The hot summer sun dissipates an inadequate rainfall; dry-land farming is done, but extensive agriculture and the growing of winter vegetables is profitable only where there is irrigation.

San Antonio and Laredo are the most important commercial centers of South Texas, with San Antonio by far the dominant city. San Antonio rises from the prairies where the Gulf and Rio Grande Plains merge and end against the fraying limestone formations of the Balcones Scarp. Like Rome, it straddles low hills; it is dotted with glens and springs. The natural beauty and mild climate made the spot an oasis to Spanish explorers coming northward out of the Mexican deserts in the late seventeenth century. They found wood and water and good river bottom soils, and the Spanish planted a string of missions here, along the headwaters of the San Antonio River. The first, San Antonio de Valero, named in honor of both St. Anthony of Padua and the reigning viceroy of New Spain, and its companion fort, the Royal Presidio of San Antonio de Bexar, were founded in 1718.

By 1731 permanent settlers were induced from the Canary Islands; their descendants are still here. San Antonio became the capital of Spanish Texas; however, by the early nineteenth century it had only some 3,000 inhabitants and a few good buildings. Then it was caught up in the bloody events of the Mexican War for Independence and the Texas Revolution; San Antonio was twice captured by Mexican armies in the Texas–Mexican skirmishes of 1842. The most fought-over city on the North American continent, San Antonio is easily the most "historic" place in Texas.

In later years the city became an inland port for the Mexican trade, a jumping-off place for California on the transcontinental run, the military headquarters for the Texas frontier, and a mercantile and banking center for surrounding farming communities and ranching empires. It grew into a large city — in 1900 it was the biggest in Texas — and a favorite retirement spot.

Surpassed by Dallas and Houston in the oil and industrial age, San Antonio has remained a great city despite the lack of industry and local oil business. It is the third largest city in Texas and the eleventh largest in the United States. The secret of its charm, admitted by every visitor, is a successful blending of the old and new. New towers rise beside old walls, but the walls and ancient plazas have never lost their feeling of historicity. Successive waves of German, French, Southern, and Mexican immigrants into the old Spanish town have created a unique confluence of cultures — cultures that bend and blend but never quite absorb each other. Old and cosmopolitan, San Antonio, like Boston, New Orleans, and San Francisco, is often described as one of America's four unique cities.

Fiesta San Antonio: Built around the anniversary of the Battle of San Jacinto, which assured Texas independence on April 21, 1836, Fiesta Week, with parades — the Battle of Flowers parade has been held since 1892 — ceremonies, block parties, and carnivals throughout the downtown, is one of the city's major attractions.

San Antonio River: The spring-fed stream courses through the entire city, its banks covered by lush subtropical trees and shrubs. Barges are available for sightseeing or for a Mexican dinner accompanied by musicians.

River Walk: San Antonio is probably most remembered by visitors for its river. In the 1920s businessmen wanted to pave it over and convert it into a sewer; fortunately for posterity, however, some preservation-minded ladies prevailed. The lovely riverside has been attractively developed with walks, shops, and open-air restaurants, all with a very Latin or southern European look.

The lights of San Antonio: To borrow from the French saying about Paris, it can be said that every Texan has two homes: his own and San Antonio. New–old San Antonio is much what it has always been: an oasis up from the dusty plains; the largest military center in Texas with five major bases; a banking, sales and distribution center for a wide region. As the most historic city in Texas, and perhaps also the most beautiful, with its blending of old and new and its laid-back style, it has become a major tourist attraction and a national retirement center.

San Antonio for better or worse has little industry, although a new wave of high-tech enterprise is gathering along the Austin–San Antonio corridor. The $3.3 billion federal payroll is vital but of gradually decreasing importance as the city grows.

The famed River Walk beside the stream that meanders through the downtown, the sun-drenched plazas, the Alamo, and the annual festivals that celebrate anything and everything from Texas Independence to music and folklife — San Antonians are always ready to party — draw hundreds of thousands of visitors from around the state and nation.

The Alamo: The most famous site in Texas, the Alamo is more than the Shrine of Texas Liberty — it is a world shrine, where millions of Americans and peoples from foreign lands have come to honor the heroism of the 180-odd men who died defending it against overwhelming odds in 1836, preparing the way for the Texan victory at San Jacinto. The defenders died to the last man; to this day no one knows where they were buried.

The Alamo was not originally a fortress. The surviving structures are the facade of the mission church and convent of San Antonio de Valero. The church was erected in 1758. After the mission was secularized by the Spanish crown, a troop of cavalry from San José y Santiago del Alamo in Mexico preempted the grounds, converting the convent into a barracks and conferring its name —the Alamo troop — on it for posterity.

Used as a sometime Army quartermaster depot, store, and warehouse in the nineteenth century, the grounds were saved from being razed for a hotel by the efforts of Clara Driscoll, daughter of a noted South Texas ranching family. In 1905, the State of Texas appointed the Daughters of the Republic of Texas to manage and maintain the shrine without cost to the public.

Four of the eighteenth-century Spanish missions survive in some form in the San Antonio area, though none has the bloody history, or fascination, of the Alamo.

King Ranch headquarters and main house on Santa Gertrudis Creek: Its brand, the Running W, may not be as well-known as that of the defunct XIT, but the King Ranch is the most famous cattle empire in the world. In 1852 Captain Richard King, a Northerner who steamboated on the Rio Grande, bought a 75,000-acre Spanish land grant on Santa Gertrudis Creek, beginning one of the great Texas legends and fortunes. The ranch once held 1.25 million acres, sprawling over Nueces, Kennedy, Kleberg and Willacy Counties along the Laguna Madre. Manager Robert Justus Kleberg married the boss's daughter, the ranch became a family corporation, and Kleberg heirs have held all the shares since.

The ranch pioneered in developing suitable stock for tick-infested South Texas. Eventually Indian Brahmans were crossed with shorthorns, resulting in the famed Santa Gertrudis breed. Fallen on hard times, the ranch was saved in the 1930s by the largest oil lease ever negotiated in the United States, and major finds of natural gas and petroleum. Today King Ranch Inc. is a vast, diversified enterprise, raising thoroughbred horses, supplying feedlot steers for McDonald's hamburgers, as well as having interests in banking and East Texas timberlands. It owns huge ranching interests in Australia, Brazil, Argentina, and Venezuela as well as properties in several American states. And the ranch is working on its brand-name recognition, with a line of leather goods stamped with the Running W.

BILL ELZEY

King Ranch headquarters, Santa Gertrudis division: The King Ranch is the only cattle spread in Texas that still maintains the aura of a feudal kingdom. Now reduced to 825,000 acres behind 1,500 miles of fences, this private empire is still a world to itself, jealously guarded. It is a vast game preserve with its own wildlife manager. The brush abounds with deer, duck, quail and antelope. Exxon operates a refinery on ranch property, but no one entering the ranch may carry firearms, liquor, or fishing equipment. Housing, a church, and schools are provided for ranch employees; some families have worked here for generations. Times, however, are changing; now the sons and daughters of cowhands leave to become doctors, lawyers, and politicians.

Where the deer and the nilgai play: Texas cattle share the range with wild turkey, antelope, deer, bobcats, javelinas or peccaries, eagles, and buzzards — a protected bird — and also some strange non-native animals such as nilgai. Several species of African and Indian birds and antelope as well as European boars have been transplanted to the Texas plains, where they are generally known as "exotics." The nilgai *(Bolselaphus tragocomelus)* is a large antelope native to the Indian subcontinent, whose name means "blue cow" in Hindi. The adult animal stands 4½ feet high at the shoulder and is 6½ feet long; the male is bluish-grey with short horns, while the female is tawny-colored and hornless.

Many South Texas ranches have imported exotics. Sometimes these may be hunted; primarily they are for show. Most large Texas ranches are in effect game management areas. Hunting leases are an important source of income, but species and numbers are carefully monitored, and the harvesting of game is much like the marketing of cattle. In the 1982–3 season 337,600 whitetail deer were killed in Texas, together with 53,500 wild turkey and 18,900 javelina pigs. Hunting of native game animals is regulated by the state; the control of exotics is left to landowners.

Laredo on the Rio Grande: All border towns are similar; each is unique. But all live in symbiosis with sister cities across the international boundary. Laredo was founded by Spanish settlers in 1755. Because of Indian raids they moved to the south bank of the river and established Nuevo or "New" Laredo. But a town eventually took root on the Texas side, and when Texas jurisdiction was extended here in 1846 the population numbered about 2,000. It has now grown to some 90,000, while Nuevo Laredo is still larger. The inhabitants of both cities are overwhelmingly Mexican in background, and Laredo is an important retail center for much of northern Mexico. Sixty percent of all import–export trade between the United States and Mexico passes through here. The first international bridge supplanted the ferry in 1889; now millions of tourists from both sides cross the two auto and pedestrian bridges.

Laredo is tied to the economy of Mexico, booming or suffering accordingly. Nuevo Laredo similarly depends on the Yankee dollar; the new race-track was strategically situated beside the border in the hope of luring aficionados from Texas, where most forms of betting are illegal.

BILL ELLZEY

Race track, Nuevo Laredo. (This is on Mexican side.)

The Lower Rio Grande Valley

"Snowbirds" at Harlingen, Rio Grande Valley: The Lower Rio Grande Valley (called the Valley) is actually the broad delta of the Rio Grande River, which defines the border of Texas as it flows eastward here into the Gulf. The Texas side of the "Valley" is about 60 miles across from north to south, and its maximum length east to west is 160 miles if it is measured from Falcon Lake in Starr County to the mouth of the river. But while Falcon Lake and Starr County are usually officially included in the Valley, that western portion is far more like the Brush Country of South Texas than part of the peculiar lower Valley ecology. The Valley has rich alluvial soils, water from the Rio Grande for irrigation, and a semi-tropical climate, where — although periodic freezes can devastate the region — the growing season reaches 341 days, and some years there is no frost at all. This creates a distinct climatic and ecological area at the tip of Texas, the "Magic Valley," which has become a great agribusiness and tourism center. The fruit and vegetable capital of the state, with major cotton and grain crops, the Valley is visited by thousands of Northern "snowbirds," mostly from the Midwest, who seem to arrive and depart with the migrating geese. Many tourists fly in, but thousands of others come in recreational vehicles to winter among the palm trees.

BILL ELLZEY

Below

World War II Memorial, Marine Military Academy, Harlingen.

Right Rebel Field, Headquarters of the Confederate Air Force: Yes, there *is* a Confederate Air Force, appropriately based near the late Confederacy's southernmost point. The CAF was founded by World War II pilots who wanted to preserve and fly the aircraft of the last great war. The CAF Flying Museum now has the only collection of World War II planes in existence, almost all in flying condition. And the Confederate Air Force provided most of the planes and pilots for such movies as "Tora, Tora, Tora!" and "The Battle of Britain" — no one else had Zeros, Spitfires, and Hawker Hurricanes, or wanted to fly them in simulated combat.

There is only one rank in the CAF: full colonel. The headquarters is the Octagon, and the motto, *Semper Mint Julep*. A mythical Col. Jethro C. Culpepper is the leader — but, yes, Yankees can join up too.

Harlingen: Harlingen is a hub city of 43,500 in the center of the Rio Grande Valley, typical of the area's "new towns." In 1900 almost all the Valley was still covered with dense, jungle-like brush; the land required vision, irrigation and drainage techniques, and capital investment for development. Pioneer developer and industrialist Lon C. Hill founded a town with his plantation here in 1901. First known as "Lon Hill's town" or "Six-Shooter Junction" (early in the century there were bandit raids and most men went armed), Harlingen was eventually named for the ancestral home in Holland of Uriah Lott, early promoter and railroad man.

The bandits, if not all the six-shooters, are gone, and Harlingen is a mid-Valley center for agribusiness, distribution, and tourism.

Carnival during Charro Days, Brownsville.

Brownsville: The Valley's largest city, Brownsville is an old border town of 85,000 with a diversified economy based on retailing, agriculture, tourism, and the sea. Twenty-two miles up the Rio Grande from the Gulf, it began as Fort Brown, named for an American soldier killed here in the skirmishes that precipitated the Mexican War. In the 1850s Brownsville was one of the largest towns in Texas, a port of entry for Mexico connected by steamboats and rails with Boca Chica on the Gulf. During the Civil War it was much fought over by Union and Confederate forces as the center of the Southern cotton trade. When rails reached Laredo and Boca Chica Pass silted up in the 1880s, the area stagnated until the turn of the century, which brought the railroads, large-scale irrigated farming, and newcomers. The land boom of the 1920s was followed by the development of shipping, tourism, seafood processing, and manufacturing.

Just across the river from the major Mexican city of Matamoros, Brownsville is a shopping center for northern Mexico and is seriously affected by the twists of that economy. The city, predominantly Mexican in background, celebrates its borderlands heritage with a pre-Lenten festival, Charro Days (parades, rodeos, costume balls and general carnival), and Fiesta Internacional, honoring Mexico's independence day in September.

Irrigated fields, Rio Grande Valley.

GEORGE HALL

Below Private estate, near Harlingen.

BILL ELLZEY

Right Citrus orchards, Rio Grande Valley.

GEORGE HALL

Ninety percent of the Valley's agribusiness income comes from orchards and irrigated croplands. Texas red grapefruit, sold under various names, is considered by many to be the best grapefruit produced in the United States. On Christmas 1983, however, the worst freeze in Valley history — the first citrus-damaging freeze in more than 20 years — destroyed most of the crop and killed many trees. Production will not be resumed for some years.

Below Orange grove, Rio Grande Valley.

BILL ELLZEY

GEORGE HALL

Above Irrigated fields, Rio Grande Valley.

Resaca, Rio Grande Valley: For many hundreds of years the Rio Grande, meandering in snakelike twists across a flat delta that rises only about one foot per mile inland from the Gulf, has been working its way southward. This southern progress has been largely halted by dams and other measures — after all, the international boundary with Mexico is at stake. But the course of centuries has left the Texas side of the delta dotted with countless oxbow lakes, which the early Spanish settlers called *resacas*. Each resaca was cut off as the river found new and shorter channels in times of flood; from the air the process is immediately apparent across the entire Valley.

Many of the very old former river beds have dried up or turned to swale, but most of the newer ones serve a vital function as reservoirs into which fresh water can be turned or pumped from the Rio Grande. They are used for both farm irrigation and cities' water supplies. As former river banks, resaca lands are generally the richest in the region, and resaca-side property is avidly sought for homes and estates, where the water provides scenic beauty as well as fishing and recreation.

Left Port Isabel, with Padre Island causeway in the background: Port Isabel, a fishing village of 3,800 at the southern end of the Laguna Madre, shares with Brownsville the world's greatest fleet of shrimp boats. It is also a deepwater port, ranking 12th in Texas, and the busy gateway to South Padre Island to which it is connected by a causeway across the bay. The fishing here is said to be the best on any of America's three coasts. Despite its distance from large centers of population more and more sportsmen seek it out. Bay fishing is good year-round, though more species run in the Gulf in summer months. Major tournaments are held at Port Isabel–Padre Island every August, and fishermen pursue everything from giant marlin to pompano and Spanish mackerel and Southern flounder. On any given day, however, they all may prove refractory.

BILL ELLZEY

Above Shipyard, Port Brownsville: Emulating Houston and Corpus Christi, Brownsville became a deepwater seaport in 1935 through the dredging of an inland waterway from Brazos Pass on the Gulf. The port is an international free-trade zone and is the ninth busiest on the Texas coast. It is also home to the largest shrimping fleet in the United States.
Industries dot the Brownsville ship channel. Here the Marathon–LeTourneau Shipyard turns out the famed "Texas towers" that are used for offshore oil drilling. Some platforms manufactured here have been towed as far as the North Sea off Scotland.

Right Beach and breakers, South Padre Beach: Only now receiving worldwide recognition, the pristine beach at South Padre Island is one of the finest anywhere in the world. And here Texas ends, in the primal sea where it all began.

Above Laguna Madre: The "mother lagoon" of the Texas coast is a long, shallow basin that runs south from Corpus Christi between Padre Island and the mainland for more than 100 miles, emptying into the Gulf at Brazos Pass near Port Isabel. Narrow in places, widening out into sprawling flats and basins in others, the Laguna Madre serves as the eastern fence line for some great South Texas and Valley ranches. The shoreline and islands grow mostly sparse salt grasses, but these have supported some cattle since Spanish times. Most of the bays and shoreline are remote, reachable only by boat. Small isles dot the shallow saltwater flats, green with saline vegetation and surrounded by crystal waters, through which vari-colored bottom muds and sands appear in vivid contrasts and create the effect of tropic seas. The Laguna Madre is a sportsman's paradise, swarming with spawning fish in spring and summer, teeming with waterfowl in fall. Normally inhabited only by lonely cattle which leave their hoofprints upon the sand, the sand banks here and there reveal a hunter's hut or "blind."

Map of Texas

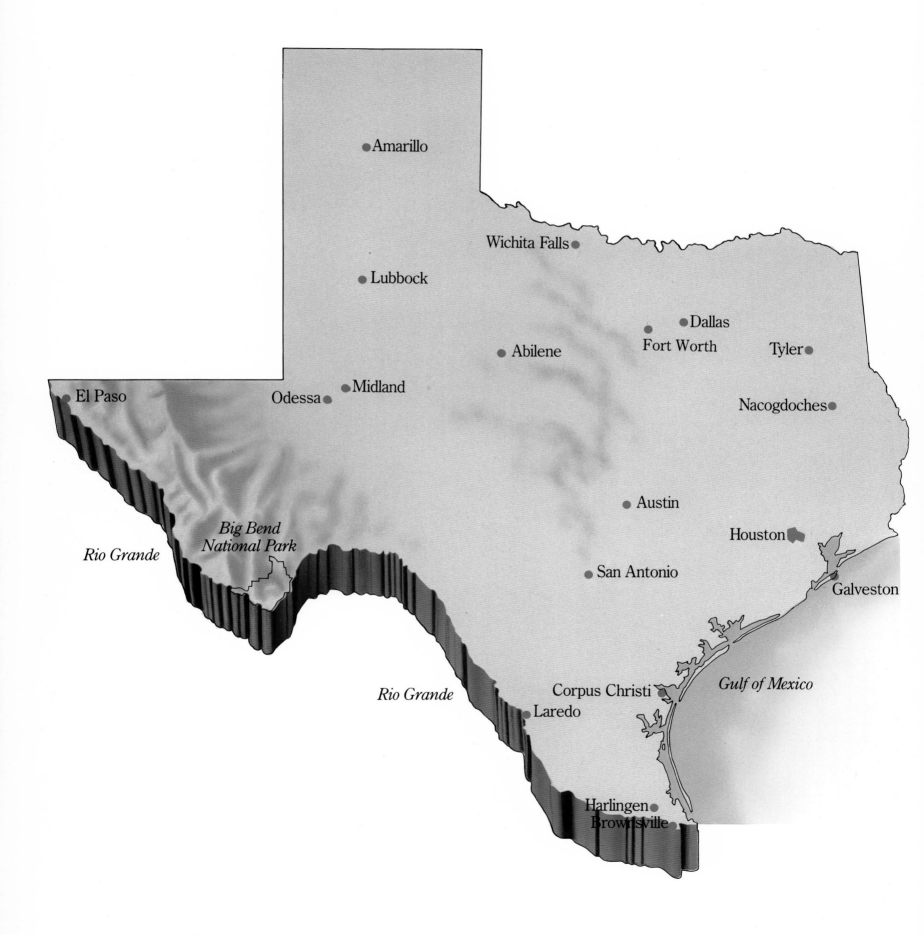

- ●Amarillo
- Wichita Falls●
- ●Lubbock
- ●Dallas
- Fort Worth●   Tyler●
- ●Abilene
- El Paso●   Odessa● ●Midland   Nacogdoches●
- *Big Bend*
  National Park
- *Rio Grande*
- ●Austin
- Houston●
- San Antonio●
- Galveston
- *Rio Grande*   Corpus Christi●   *Gulf of Mexico*
- Laredo●
- Harlingen●
- Brownsville●